PLANTS & GARDENS
BROOKLYN BOTANIC GARDEN RECORD

TREES
A GARDENER'S GUIDE

VOL. 48, No. 3, AUTUMN 1992

HANDBOOK #132

FOREWORD

Trees are the backbone of the garden. True, they are important structural elements in the landscape, but as living organisms they are much more. They provide the cooling shade that tempts us to linger in the garden on a hot summer day. Street trees make our cities more habitable by giving visual relief to the asphalt landscape, and at the same time they help cut down on noise and purify the air. On a global scale, trees are vital for oxygen regeneration.

We ask a lot of every tree we plant, so it behooves us to choose wisely and plant carefully. To help gardeners, landscapers, nurserymen, urban foresters and planners analyze a planting site and select the best tree for its location, BBG offers this new handbook of 100 excellent trees for a wide range of landscape situations.

The trees described in this volume come highly recommended by expert horticulturists across the country. Many thanks to the following people for their help in compiling the list:

Robert Breunig, Desert Botanical Garden; Michael A. Dirr, University of Georgia; Harrison L. Flint, Purdue University; Edward R. Hasselkus, University of Wisconsin; Allen R. Howard, Los Angeles State and County Arboretum; Arthur H. Ode, Nebraska Statewide Arboretum; Harold Pellet, Minnesota Landscape Arboretum; Ken Slump, Denver Botanic Garden; and Shannon Smith, Missouri Botanical Garden.

We hope this handbook will inspire you to seek out your own finest 100 trees — and to plant at least a few of them.

JUDITH D. ZUK
GUEST EDITOR

Consider bark texture when selecting a tree.
At left is *Stewartia pseudocamellia*.

SELECTING THE RIGHT TREE

BY PAUL W. MEYER

When gardeners select and buy a tree, we rarely give the purchase the same careful consideration that we give an automobile or other major purchase. Though its initial cost may not be so great, a tree is an investment that can satisfy a family for generations.

Choosing a tree can be a challenging task, but it's easy to cut the project down to size by following the suggestions below. The best way to begin is with a few simple observations. Stand at the site that you have chosen for your tree. Look around. In midsummer, would it be in the open or in the shade? Would there be full sun all day? Are there structures or other large plants nearby?

Next, look at the trees growing in your community. What are they? How big are they? How long have they been there? Are they holding up well to environmental

PAUL W. MEYER *is Director of the Morris Arboretum of the University of Pennsylvania.*

Left:
Young *Betula nigra* 'Heritage' in spring.

stress? And, are they attractive and appropriate for the site that you have in mind? Observe as many trees as possible throughout the community, visit local botanic gardens and arboreta and, finally, get advice from reputable nurseries. This will help insure that your arboreal investment yields long-lasting dividends.

The Science of Choosing Your Tree

To be vigorous and long-lived, a tree species must be well adapted to its site. Climate and soil are the most important considerations. Tree species vary in their adaptability to environmental conditions. Before planting, know the temperature extremes in your area. A hardiness zone map (see page 93) can serve as a guide. Well-adapted species will tolerate both extremes of winter cold and summer heat. Similarly, a well-adapted tree will be suitable to the soil and light conditions of the site. It is important to know the relative alkalinity or acidity, or pH, of the soil. This can be measured using a simple kit available in garden centers or through your local county cooperative extension agent. Some trees such as pin oak (*Quercus palustris*) require acidic soil, or a low pH. If the soil is neutral (a pH of 7) or alkaline (a pH above 7), the leaves of the pin oak will become yellow and chlorotic. Even when soils are generally acidic, alkalinity may be a problem near foundations and pavement, where calcium leaches from the mortar and raises the pH. Trees such as bur oak (*Quercus macrocarpa*) are well adapted to alkaline soil and should be used in these instances.

The relative availability of water in the soil is also critical to the tree's health. Both too much and too little water can be a problem. Observe the existing soil conditions. If the soil is sandy and dries quickly after a rain, use drought-tolerant species such as turkish hazel (*Corylus colurna*) or black oak (*Quercus velutina*). If the soil is heavy and puddles of water persist after a rain, a tree species native to flood plains or swamp

Left: The native dogwood, *Cornus florida*, produces a white cloud of blossoms in spring. Above: The filigreed leaf form of Japanese maple, *Acer palmatum*.

edges such as river birch (*Betula nigra*), swamp white oak (*Quercus bicolor*) or red maple (*Acer rubrum*) is most appropriate. Also remember that all trees require at least some direct sunlight but some, such as dogwood (*Cornus florida*) tolerate more shade than others.

Our increasing awareness of the danger of toxic sprays is making more evident than ever the importance of using trees that are naturally resistant to both insects and diseases. For example, some crabapple cultivars such as 'Hopa' are highly susceptible to disease while others such as 'Donald Wyman' are highly resistant. Some of the best disease-resistant plants are listed in the encyclopedia section of this handbook.

Disease and insect resistance can also be influenced by the site. Often, if a plant is poorly adapted to its particular growing conditions, it may well be biologically stressed and become more susceptible to insects and diseases. A plant in an appropriate site is more likely to be resistant to insect and disease attack. This is all the more reason to do some research before buying a tree.

Size and Habit

Imagine your tree ten or 20 years from

Fruits provide seasonal color and also attract wildlife to your garden. The bright orange-red fruits of 'Winter King' hawthorn persist long into winter.

now. Will it crowd its neighbors? Will it shade your sun-loving vegetable garden? When selecting a tree it is important to know its ultimate size and shape. Far too often, trees quickly outgrow the available space and must be removed or severely pruned at great expense. But there are trees for all situations. For a small, confined area, small, open-growing trees with fibrous root systems such as the sweet bay magnolia (*Magnolia virginiana*) are a good choice. Likewise, avoid planting large canopy trees under utility wires. Instead, select small understory trees such as European hornbeam (*Carpinus betulus*).

Next, consider the growth rate of desirable trees. Fast-growing species are often tempting, particularly if there are no other trees on the property. Generally speaking, fast-growing trees are weak-wooded, subject to breakage and often short-lived. Rather than selecting a fast-growing, weedy tree such as silver maple (*Acer saccharinum*), it is usually better to select a slower-growing tree that is well-adapted to the site. With regular watering and fertilization, even a reputed slow-grower such as red oak (*Quercus rubra*) can grow three feet per year. Your patience will be rewarded ten to 15 years from now when a slower-growing tree continues to be a valued asset in the garden rather than an unwanted nuisance.

The overall form of the tree is also a major consideration. Upright, ascending trees such as Japanese zelkova (*Zelkova serrata*) are useful along roads, paths or close to buildings. Broad spreading trees are most useful on an open lawn where extensive shade is desired. Many cultivated varieties of the commonly planted species have been selected for their varying forms. Red maple is a striking example. Its cultivar 'Armstrong' has a narrow columnar form; 'Autumn Flame' is rounded; 'Bowhall' has an upright oval to pyramidal form; and 'Gerling' is broadly pyramidal. Choose the cultivar that best suits your needs.

The Art of Choosing Your Tree

Now that you have considered the cultural requirements of your tree, you can turn with pleasure to the aesthetic considerations. Think about what you might enjoy most: distinctive foliage? Flowers? Fruit in winter?

If light dappled shade is what you want, a fine-textured tree such as thornless honeylocust (*Gleditsia triacanthos* var. *inermis*) is appropriate. Its finely cut, fernlike leaves allow dappled sunlight to penetrate the canopy to the ground. Similarly, if you're looking for a coarser texture or heavier shade, the common sugar maple (*Acer saccharum*) is a good choice. Fine-textured trees have smaller leaves which create less of a volume when they fall

in the autumn, a vital consideration in some urban areas.

If you want a more dynamic landscape, be sure to include flowering trees, which dramatically brighten the landscape. When choosing flowering trees, consider how the flower color blends with other colors in the landscape. Note the time of flower and the color of adjacent trees and shrubs as well as the dominant colors in nearby buildings. Take care to avoid clashing colors and plan for pleasing combinations and an interesting sequence of flowers in your garden. Too often, only early-spring flowering trees like crabapples and flowering cherries are planted. Late-flowering trees like goldenrain tree (*Koelreuteria paniculata*) and Chinese scholar tree (*Sophora japonica*) are welcome additions because they bloom in summer when few other trees are in flower.

Tree foliage also adds color to the landscape. Trees such as the purple-leaved European beech and purple-leaved plum are popular. When used indiscriminately, they can be jarring. But when used judiciously, they can be a welcome accent. The secret is to use colored foliage sparingly, as a focal point.

Fruits, too, can provide seasonal color and also attract birds and other wildlife to your garden. The winter king hawthorn (*Crataegus viridis* 'Winter King') is one favorite with bright orange-red fruits which persist long into the winter. Its fruits can be attractive for a period of up to three or four months while its flowers typically last no longer than a week. It is a wonderful sight to see the fruits of this hawthorn being stripped off in late winter or early spring by robins and cedar waxwings migrating north.

Choosing a tree is a challenge, but a potentially rewarding one. "A penny for the plant, a pound for the planting" goes the adage. Likewise, when you plant a tree, invest a penny for the plant and a pound for the *planning*.

TRANSPLANTING

&

CARE

BY EDMOND O. MOULIN

Transplanting is one of the most critical times in the life of a tree. Preparing the planting hole is of paramount importance. As the old saying goes: "Never put a two-dollar plant in a fifty-cent hole."

Before I get into the art of digging a hole and preparing the soil, however, I should mention that the first order of business is getting the tree home safely. If you are transporting the young tree, make sure you protect it from drying wind, even if the plant is dormant.

The Planting Hole

Dig the hole at least two to three times wider than the root ball. The larger the root system or the higher it is planted, the greater the width of the hole. The depth of the hole must accommodate the roots. If it is necessary to dig deeper to remove rubble or break up hardpan, firm the fill to

EDMOND O. MOULIN *is Director of Horticulture at the Brooklyn Botanic Garden.*

support the root system and prevent sinkage. Avoid compacting the soil, especially wet soil.

In good, well-drained soil, plant so that the top of the root ball is nearly level with the surrounding grade. If the soil is heavy and drainage is poor, plant so that the top of the root system is three to four inches above the surrounding grade, and dig the hole at least three feet wider than the root system.

Preparing the Soil

If the soil structure is good, you won't have to add organic matter. However, poor soil can be improved by adding compost, sphagnum peat moss or any good garden humus. Organic matter helps aerate heavy clay soils and improves water retention in sandy soils. Add ten to 30 percent organic matter.

The backfill should be good enough to encourage root growth laterally into it from the existing root system, but not so different from the undisturbed surrounding soil that it becomes an artificial container that

Left: Balled & burlaped trees are less likely to develop girdling roots than container-grown trees.

restricts future root growth. It is in the backfill that amendments recommended in your soil test, such as agricultural limestone or phosphorus, should be mixed.

Positioning

Plant so that the trunk is vertical unless you prefer a slanting style for a Japanese or naturalistic landscape. If the tree seems to be one-sided, place the more sparsely branched side to the south. If the trunk is fairly straight but the top of the tree seems to bend to one side, plant with the list into the prevailing wind or else to the north. Future growth will help to balance the tree's architecture.

Bare Root Trees

Trees up to ten feet tall and less than two inches in diameter may be sold bare root. Young trees that are not too difficult to transplant, and especially fruit trees or their ornamental relatives, are sold bare root in early spring while they are still dormant. Mail order stock is handled in this manner.

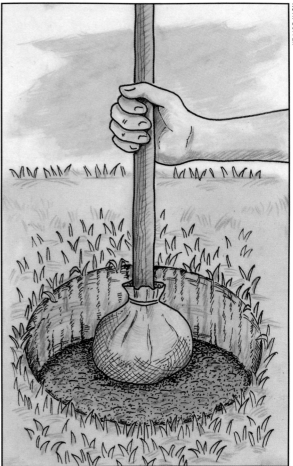

RUTH SOFFER

Dig the planting hole at least two to three times wider than the root system and just deep enough to accommodate it.

Plan to plant as early in the spring as the soil can be worked. When you receive the tree, unwrap and inspect it and determine the depth and spread of the root system. Do not allow the roots to become dry. Prune to remove broken, damaged, crossover and other roots that do not radiate out (away) from the trunk. Soak overnight in water or a slurry of mud to hydrate the tissues.

In the meantime prepare the hole and mix the backfill. Spread the roots out and start filling the hole to hold the radiating roots in place, firm lightly, and start adding water slowly, gently wiggling the tree to remove air pockets. Add soil to the settling soil using a thin dowel-rod, such as a chopstick, to work the soil into the mud around the roots and work the air bubbles out. The surface roots should be left at grade with the surrounding topography or up to three to four inches higher in poorly drained sites. In this case the roots should be covered with soil as on a mound tapered to the surrounding grade.

The "backfill" can be improved with compost or peat moss but should not differ greatly from the surrounding soil.

root mass using a sharp knife or a sharp spade. Use hand pruners to remove encircling roots that cannot be redirected.

Using the same tools, open outward the roots that grew at the base of the container. This can be safely done to halfway up the root ball. Finally, check the roots at the top of the ball to be sure there are no large roots that might girdle the trunk.

Now set the tree in the hole on a mound of soil, spreading the roots outward. Fill the hole about half full with the prepared backfill, then firm lightly. Water slowly, working in more soil using a dowel-stick to eliminate air pockets (or use the hose itself). Do not compact the soil.

Balled & Burlaped Trees

Deciduous trees that are dug while dormant can be safely planted at any time, even when in full leaf, if they are properly maintained before and after planting. B&B plants are less

Create a saucer for watering (see "Mounding the Soil" below), mulch and stake if necessary.

Container-Grown Trees

Container-grown trees can be planted at any time of the year. After removing the tree from the container, examine the root system. If the roots are fine, use a hand fork-tine cultivator to loosen the outer layer of roots which tend to mat at the sides. If the roots are heavy and encircling, make four vertical cuts at the periphery of the

likely to develop girdling roots than container-grown plants. The disadvantage of B&B stock is finding the top of the root system; the top of the ball may not be it. Cultivation practices in the nursery row may result in soil buildup over the roots, and to compound the problem the tree may have been planted deeply to begin with, leaving the top of the ball three to six inches higher than the surface roots. Unless you can feel the roots, it is impossible to determine their depth without opening the burlap. Do this with care, being sure not to cut the cord lacings. Cut out windows of burlap on the top of the ball to check. If there is excess top soil, plant accordingly (see "Planting Hole" above) and remove the excess after planting is completed.

Backfill with the prepared mix to three fourths of the way up the depth of the root ball. While watering slowly, remove the lacings from the base of the trunk and fold back the burlap into the hole. Finish planting as for container-grown stock.

Mounding the Soil

Create a "basin" for holding water by building a mound of soil three to four inches high at the outer rim of the planting site and firm it. This will help to catch rain and make watering easier.

Pruning

A bare root tree needs to be more severely top pruned than B&B or container-grown plants to compensate for root loss so that the remaining root system can adequately supply water and nutrients to the top growth. Remove any broken portions of branches. Thin out closely spaced branches and cut back lateral branches by a third. Do not cut back the central trunk or lead unless it is damaged or weakened or unless you want a low-crown tree.

Prune B&B and container-grown trees to remove broken branches below the point of injury. Remove crossing branches and, if necessary, prune back some of the laterals to balance the shape. Where possible, remove branches that form narrow-

Create a "basin" to help catch rain and make watering easier.

angle crotches with the main trunk. These V-shaped structures are inherently weak and subject to breakage in the future. Most nursery-produced trees are well pruned and do not require extensive pruning.

Staking

Newly planted trees can be uprooted by heavy winds or human actions. Stake the trunk until new roots provide the necessary anchorage. The support system should be in place only for a growing season for smaller trees and possibly up to two

Stake small trees for one growing season and larger trees for up to two years.

such as hemp, around the trunk in a figure eight and secure it to the stake.

For larger trees, drive three stakes vertically outside the area of the root system. Use pliant wire put through a short piece of rubber hose (to protect the trunk), then cross it in a figure eight and twist the wire around the stake tight enough so that the wire won't slip.

Watering

When it has been seven to ten days since a good soaking rain, fill the basin with water. Allow to soak in and fill it again. Water deeply when necessary for at least the first growing season.

Mulching

Apply a three- to four-inch layer of non-compacting organic mulch within the saucer area. Shredded hardwood, oak leaves, pine needles or pine bark are all suitable. Mulch reduces water loss from the soil, keeps the soil temperature stable and discourages weeds.

years for larger trees.

Air movements flex the tree trunk, building caliper (width) and strength. For this reason, it is sometimes recommended that trees be staked low down on the trunk. Short stakes, however, can be hazardous, because people are more apt to trip over them. What's more, higher stakes help protect the tree from damage by cars, bikes and the like.

One stake driven down close to the trunk may be enough for bare root trees. Tie a strip of burlap or soft organic cord,

Fertilizing

When new growth appears, apply a liquid fertilizer diluted according to the manufacturer's directions. Repeat once a month until mid-July. Never fertilize dry soil (even if the fertilizer is diluted in water).

The following spring when you fertilize the lawn, be sure to share the broadcast with the tree. But be sure not to use combined herbicide/fertilizer formulations!

URBAN TREES

BY NINA BASSUK

With all of urban America's social problems, why should we even consider the plight of trees? Quite simply, green space makes the urban environment bearable. Trees and other vegetation help purify and oxygenate the air and also play a role in replenishing groundwater supplies and reducing storm-water runoff. By providing shade and blocking wind, urban trees also help conserve energy. Mass plantings reduce noise and glare. Urban vegetation provides critical habitat for birds. Properly placed trees and shrubs also screen unsightly views and beautify the city. By helping to create a unique identity for a neighborhood, trees even help preserve its economic base.

And yet we take street trees for granted. Recent surveys indicate that in cities four trees are dying for every one planted, that the average life-span of a "downtown" city tree is *seven years* and that cities are only 40 to 50 percent planted. Unless these trends are reversed our cities will eventually become treeless.

NINA BASSUK *is Director of the Urban Horticulture Institute at Cornell University.*

Left: Restricted root growth is a major problem for city trees.

ELVIN McDONALD

Street microclimates can be substantially hotter and less humid than other environments, causing severe water deficits.

Why is street tree mortality so high?

All plants have six basic needs: water, nutrients, light, a certain range of temperature, oxygen and carbon dioxide. If any one of these falls below a certain threshold for a particular plant, the plant will begin to decline and eventually die. When trees are growing below an acceptable level they are experiencing stress — either "abiotic," caused by deficiencies in the physical environment, or "biotic," caused by insects and disease. Trees in the urban environment have to deal with a disproportionately high number of abiotic stresses because they were added as an afterthought to the built environment. By definition, road and sidewalk construction requires that soils be highly compacted to prevent subsidence. When trees are added to this environment their roots are often restricted by the compacted soil on all sides, almost as if they were in a container. This containerization,

which can also be caused by underground utilities and buildings, restricts root growth and therefore limits the trees' catchment area for water and nutrients. Compaction also restricts water drainage, which can displace oxygen in the root zone for so long that roots die. Poor drainage probably destroys urban trees faster than any other factor. The prevalence of above-ground planters in areas where in-ground planting is impossible compounds the problem of containerization by exposing roots to potentially very low temperatures in winter and very high temperatures in summer.

The problem of restricted root growth is compounded by high-pH soils and de-icing salts. It is now recognized that run-off from concrete and asphalt into tree-planting areas, combined with limestone-containing building rubble incorporated with the street "soil," raises soil pH. Alkaline soils prevent essential micronutrients such as iron, man-

T · R · E · E · S
THAT TOLERATE
ENVIRONMENTAL STRESS

D = DRY; A = ALKALINE; W = WET/POORLY DRAINED; S = SALT

Acer campestre (Hedge maple)– S

Acer platanoides (Norway maple)– S

Acer pseudoplatanus (Plane tree)– S

Alnus glutinosa (European alder)– W

Betula nigra (River birch)– W

Caragana arborescens (Siberian peashrub)– S

Celtis occidentalis (Common hackberry)– D

Corylus colurna (Turkish hazel)– D

Crataegus species (Hawthorn)– D

Eucommia ulmoides (Hardy rubber tree)– D

Fraxinus pennsylvanica (Green ash)– W

Ginkgo biloba (Ginkgo)– D

Koelreuteria paniculata (Goldenrain tree)– D

Nyssa sylvatica (Tupelo)– W

Platanus x *acerifolia* (London plane)– W

Quercus bicolor (Swamp white oak)– W

Quercus muhlenbergii (Chinkapin oak)– D

Quercus rubra (Red oak)– S

Robinia pseudoacacia (Black locust)– S

Sophora japonica (Japanese pagodatree)– D, S

Syringa reticulata (Japanese tree lilac)– D

Taxodium distichum (Bald cypress)— W

Ulmus parvifolia (Lacebark elm)– D

ganese and zinc from being taken up by many of our typical street trees, such as *Acer rubrum* (red maple), *Quercus palustris* (pin oak) and *Acer saccharum* (sugar maple). When these nutrients, which are necessary for the synthesis of chlorophyll, are deficient, leaves become chlorotic and turn yellow. Lack of chlorophyll in turn decreases the trees' ability to utilize carbon dioxide, light and water in the process of photosynthesis which is fundamental to plant growth.

Salt can be another factor which limits a tree's ability to take up water or kills leaves outright when levels of sodium and chloride become toxic. During bad winters it has been reported that 80 tons of de-icing salts are applied to each lane mile of Chicago's freeways.

Above ground the environment can also be harsh. Trees have evolved to grow in groups and thereby shade each other; however, the typical way that street trees are planted, singly in rows 30 to 40 feet apart, leaves them exposed to reflected and reradiated heat from building facades, car tops, concrete and asphalt. A study we completed on Columbus Avenue in New York City in 1985 documented that the street microclimate could be substantially hotter — up to 22 degrees F hotter in one instance — than the official temperature reading at a nearby park; on that August day, the official air temperature was 86 degrees F, yet it was 108 degrees F on the street! Aggravating the already bad situation were the 30 percent lower humidities that were also detected, giving rise to an environment which causes the leaves to lose water rapidly. A high rate of water loss from the leaves combined with a restricted root system and vast acreages of impervious pavement limiting the root zone's access to precipitation can cause severe water deficits.

So far in this discussion of abiotic

stresses, I have not mentioned air pollution. And interestingly enough, contrary to popular belief we rarely see symptoms of air pollution injury except in cities such as Los Angeles which are noted for their smog. In most cities throughout the United States, air pollution does not appear to be a major source of injury to plants.

Understanding both a tree's requirements and the environmental conditions commonly found within a city makes proper plant choices much more likely.

Although the environmental stresses mentioned above can be found in all cities, each planting area is unique and must be assessed individually. The urban environment is in fact not one environment but a variety of microclimates both above and below ground. You need only look at the non-uniform growth of identical cultivars planted in a row to see evidence of vastly different conditions within a short distance. It is the proper analysis of the limitations and opportunities at each planting area which will enable you to make proper plant selections.

Assessing the Site

The first thing to do is to make sure you are within your legal rights. Many cities have ordinances restricting where and what you may plant. If you are planting on a state road or near a railway, still other easements and restrictions may apply.

Structural Factors

Check out the planting site for structures, such as buildings, subways, roads, sidewalks, utilities, street lights, signs, heat-producing vents and street furniture. Note those that could physically and physiologically restrict your tree's canopy and root growth.

Soil Factors

The most critical of all soil tests is the one that determines the soil's drainage capabilities. Look for gray- or rust-colored mottling of the soil, which may indicate poor drainage. Pockets of standing water after a rain are another sign of problems.

You can do a simple drainage test by digging to where the roots will be, filling the hole with water and timing how quickly it drains. Anything less than one inch per hour warrants some remedial action.

You should also test soil fertility and especially pH, which determines whether or not nutrients will be available to the plant. If de-icing salts are a potential problem, have the lab test salinity levels as well. Take samples for this test during late fall, winter or early spring. Samples taken during late spring and summer rarely show salt buildup because spring rains leach salts out of the soil. The best way to confirm a salt problem is in summer, when you can take foliar samples to test for sodium and chloride buildup directly in the leaves.

By doing a little digging, determine the depth and volume of usable soil. You will want to locate underground utilities and other barriers to root growth. Because soils in urban areas rarely have a normal soil profile, you need to know where the solid or compacted layers and rubble are. These not only block root growth, but also slow or prevent drainage.

Existing Vegetation

The identity and condition of existing vegetation on the site can provide clues about site conditions. So called "indicator species" can tell you what may or may not do well there. Some examples are sugar maples, red oaks and hickories, indicating well-drained soil. Sycamores and tuliptrees naturally grow in moist soils while tupelo, willows and swamp white oak grow in poorly drained, wet soils. Be aware, however, that construction alters soils so that they will be much different from those at nearby undisturbed areas.

Pay attention to the condition of existing vegetation. Are leaves showing premature

Group trees in open islands whenever possible, where root growth is less restricted and the trees shade each other, moderating the deleterious effects of reflected light and radiated heat.

fall coloration? Are they chlorotic or are leaf margins dying back? These symptoms can indicate drought, high pH or salt damage.

Microclimate

Check out the sun and shade patterns on your site. Most trees need full sun, although some will tolerate partial shade.

Determine which USDA hardiness zone the site is in (see page 93). Analyze specific site conditions to see how they might modify the macroclimate. For example, a protected courtyard may be half a zone warmer because surrounding buildings offer wind protection and radiate heat. On the other hand, heavy prevailing winds or above-ground planters may expose trees to lower-than-normal temperatures.

Functional Considerations

Note pedestrian traffic patterns on your site. Will people actually walk over your planting area? Is there a likelihood that vehicular traffic will damage the plantings?

This is the time to make a mental note of the following as well: Are there any plants growing on the site? Are they plants you want to keep? Is the site currently unplantable? How much will you have to do to improve it? Could redesigning the site improve it? If you decide to plant, which are the most suitable species? You may decide to plant nothing or even to remove existing vegetation.

Plant Selection

The next step is to choose plants that will work on the site. Unfortunately, some city foresters have been overly concerned with finding the "perfect urban tree" — one that can withstand the entire range of urban environmental assaults. The original candidate was the American elm, *Ulmus americana*, which was so widely planted that its demise due to Dutch elm disease devastated many urban areas. As recently as 1971, it was estimated that 45 percent of all street trees in Chicago were elms. Planting all one kind of tree (known as a monoculture) does not make sense in the long run, as we are finding out with the 1960's "elm replacement" tree the honeylocust, *Gleditsia triacanthos*. It too is a tough tree, tolerant of drought, high soil pH and salt, and is easy to transplant. Now, however, we are seeing a buildup of insect pests on this tree (honeylocust plant bug and spider mites to name just two) which can be linked to the concentrated food supply. A diversity of trees matched to their proper site conditions is best.

Key factors to consider when determining a tree's suitability for a particular site are its adaptability to temperature, light and soil conditions. For example, pin oaks are almost guaranteed to develop chlorosis in alkaline soils. You will be setting yourself up for failure if that's what you select for such a site. Characteristics such as form and tendency to litter sidewalks with fruit or spent flowers are other considerations.

Another important factor to consider is seed source. A red maple grown from seed collected in Georgia may not do well in the Northeast. You will have to ask your supplier for this information or purchase plants directly from a nursery with a climate similar to yours.

See page 21 for a short list of trees that tolerate urban conditions.

Planting Technique

By putting more care and effort up front — in planning and planting — you can increase an urban tree's chances of survival. It is much easier to choose a suitable tree and plant it properly than to have to figure out how to rescue a poorly growing specimen later on. (See the article "Transplanting & Care.")

Size of Planting Area

In many urban areas, soil space for good root growth is one of the most limiting factors. Our research at Cornell is aimed at learning how much soil space a moderately large tree needs. At this point, our best estimate is that in the Northeast, a 30-foot tree with a 20-foot crown spread needs approximately 300 cubic feet of soil. That equals approximately a ten-by ten- by three-foot deep hole. Typically, even this minimally adequate area is not available because of curbs, sidewalks and compacted soil. Without space, a tree's growth is slow and stunted, and it never achieves its true characteristics.

Lack of rooting space is one stress that is difficult to overcome simply by selecting the right tree. However, several planting methods help increase soil volume available to the roots.

● Plant trees in continuous tree pits. Rather than separating individual planting areas for each tree, continuous pits run in a band. They usually parallel the street between the sidewalk and curb, and contain good, non-compacted soil. Trees in these sites have a much larger shared rooting space than those confined to a four- by four-foot area.

● Plant trees in large, raised planters. These are usually open to the ground on the bottom and have a raised concrete lip that diverts salt-water runoff.

● Group trees in open islands. Trees in the group shade each other. Together they moderate the deleterious effects of reflected light and radiated heat. Because soil around the trees is open, rain penetrates to the roots and there is no soil compaction from foot traffic.

● Mulch the entire planting area to reduce evaporation from the soil surface.

Although future research will undoubtedly improve our ability to select suitable trees and modify planting sites, it is possible — right now — to successfully grow an urban tree and put together the elements of a successful tree-planting program. Cities must be made to be compatible with trees or our loss will be far greater than we can imagine. 🌲

ADAPTED FROM AN ARTICLE IN THE PUBLIC GARDEN.

Trees planted in continuous pits running in a band between the sidewalk and curb have a much larger shared rooting space than those confined to cramped, separate pits.

100 TREES
FOR THE
HOME GARDEN

BY ANDREW BUNTING

ANDREW BUNTING *is Curator of Plants at Chanticleer, a 32-acre private garden in Wayne, Pennsylvania, which will soon open to the public. He previously worked at the Scott Arboretum in Swarthmore, Pennsylvania, and at Tintinhull House in England.*

A c a c i a   b a i l e y a n a
COOTAMUNDRA WATTLE, BAILEY'S MIMOSA

ROBERT M. HAYS

OUTSTANDING CHARACTERISTICS:

This 30-foot evergreen is prized for its outstanding foliage and winter flowers. The tree is covered with fragrant, bright yellow clusters of flowers from January to March. The beautiful blossoms contrast strikingly with the elegant, steel blue, feathery leaves.

HABIT AND USE:

A rapid grower, this species maintains a slender, graceful habit. As it matures it develops a round-headed crown. In southern California it is often used as a street tree. Because of its fine texture and relatively small stature it lends itself well to patio plantings as a specimen, or in masses. Its only drawbacks are its brittle wood and tendency to be short-lived.

CULTURE:

Adaptable to various soils. Grow in full sun. No serious pest or disease problems.

VARIETIES OR RELATED SPECIES:

'Purpurea' — the striking, deep purple young foliage contrasts with the older blue-green leaves.

HARDINESS ZONE

9

NATIVE HABITAT:
New South Wales, Australia

A c e r   b u e r g e r i a n u m
TRIDENT MAPLE

PAUL W. MEYER

OUTSTANDING CHARACTERISTICS:

Excellent small deciduous tree reaching 20 to 25 feet with an equal spread. The small, three-lobed, glossy green leaves turn brilliant yellow, orange and red later in the fall than many other maples. In the winter its orange-brown, exfoliating bark is particularly pleasing.

HABIT AND USE:

Averaging two feet of growth per year, the trident maple has a round habit at maturity. The small shade tree is an effective street tree because it tolerates drought, air pollution and soil compaction. For the small property it makes a picturesque patio or small shade tree. For shade trees with a diminutive stature it is unrivaled in pest resistance, adaptability and fall color. Often used as a subject for bonsai.

CULTURE:

This maple will prosper in full sun and acid soil but will also tolerate clay, loam or sand. It is pH adaptable, preferring a range of 6-7.5. It also tolerates drought, salt, air pollution and soil compaction and suffers from no serious pest or disease problems.

HARDINESS ZONE

5 to 8-9

NATIVE HABITAT:
East China, Korea and Japan

A c e r   g i n n a l a
AMUR MAPLE

OUTSTANDING CHARACTERISTICS:

This slow-growing, small maple reaches an ultimate height of only 15 to 18 feet with an equal spread. In full sun the glossy, dark green leaves turn vivid yellows, oranges and reds in the fall. In the spring it is one of the first trees to leaf out. The flowers, although not showy, are extremely fragrant. In the winter the bark is a handsome gray-brown.

RUTH SOFFER

HABIT AND USE:

Often grown as a multiple-stemmed large shrub or small tree. Because of its extreme hardiness this tree is suitable for the most northerly sections of the United States. Besides cold, it tolerates shade, a variety of soils and a wide pH range. It can easily be manipulated to specific landscape uses because it responds well to heavy pruning. Effective as a container specimen, as a patio tree, in masses for screening, as a foundation planting and in mixed tree and shrub borders under a canopy of light shade.

CULTURE:

The amur maple is pH adaptable, thrives in full sun or light shade and withstands heavy pruning.

HARDINESS ZONE
3 to 8
Performs better in colder climates than in the South.

NATIVE HABITAT:
Manchuria and Japan

A c e r   g r i s e u m
PAPERBARK MAPLE

OUTSTANDING CHARACTERISTICS:

A truly outstanding small deciduous tree with unequaled ornamental bark. The trunk and stems glisten throughout the year with spectacular, exfoliating cinnamon-orange bark. In the winter it contrasts brilliantly with snow. The dark green, trifoliate leaves cast a light shade and develop excellent orange and red fall color. A slow-

JOANNE PAVIA

growing tree, it can reach 20 to 40 feet with a 15- to 25-foot spread.

HABIT AND USE:

At maturity the habit is oval to rounded. The colorful birch-like, exfoliating bark makes this tree a must in the winter garden. Grown as a single specimen or in masses of three to five, it can be accentuated with a dark evergreen background. The ultimate size makes it suitable for patios or small courtyard plantings.

CULTURE:

Tolerates sun, shade and wind but not drought or other environmental stresses. Does best in well-drained loam with a pH of 5-7.

HARDINESS ZONE
5 to 8

NATIVE HABITAT:
Western and central China

OUTSTANDING CHARACTERISTICS:

A tree for many seasons. In the spring and summer Japanese maples, which reach an ultimate height and spread of 15 to 25 feet, are adorned with elegant lobed, dark green leaves. In the fall the leaves turn variations of yellow, bronze, purple and red. In the winter the young twigs are shiny green or glaucous red to purple. The trunks are smooth and dark gray to black. The growth rate is moderate, averaging 12 to 18 inches per year. Many cultivars are available with different habits, leaf colors and shapes.

HABIT AND USE:

The artistic habit of the species is equally apparent in single- and multi-stemmed specimens. It ultimately attains a broad, rounded shape with an architectural, layered branching structure similar to that of the flowering dogwood. Japanese maples are effective as small specimen trees, accent plants, patio trees in dappled shade and, in large areas, massed multiple-stemmed trees. Like the trident

ROBERT M HAYS

maple, they make excellent bonsai.

CULTURE:

The young foliage is sensitive to cold. Thrives in dappled shade; may burn in full sun. Prefers rich, moist soils but will tolerate chalk soils.

VARIETIES OR RELATED SPECIES:

'Bloodgood' — Reaches 15 to 20 feet tall. One of the best for retaining the deep reddish-purple leaf color throughout the growing season. Excellent red autumn color.

'Dissectum Atropurpureum' — A compact, sculptural habit with twisting, architectural branches. Grows six to eight feet tall with up to twice the spread. The fernlike foliage begins purple-red, turns green by mid-summer and dazzling burnt orange in fall. One of the finest accent plants for all seasons.

'Sango Kaku' — A green-leaved form (see photo above) noted for its young stems which are a brilliant coral-red in the fall and winter. Grows to 20 to 25 feet with an equal spread.

HARDINESS ZONE
6 to 8
Performs well in zone 8 where it develops good fall color in November.

NATIVE HABITAT:
Japan, Korea and China

OUTSTANDING CHARACTERISTICS:

A successful shade tree over a broad geographic range, red maple grows 40 to 60 feet tall in cultivation. This fine specimen tree has vibrant fall color; the two- to four-inch long, dark green leaves turn brilliant shades of yellow and red. Better fall color and stronger wood than the ubiquitous silver maple, *Acer saccharinum*. The growth rate is 10 to 12 feet in five to seven years. In the wilds of northeastern North America, the red maple colors before the sugar maple. The flowers, though small, produce a rosy haze along the naked branches in spring.

HABIT AND USE:

In its youth its form is pyramidal to elliptical and eventually becomes rounded. Because of its good autumn color and extensive hardiness range the red maple is a good tree from the far north to the deep south. Effectively used as a shade tree in lawns, parks, campuses and in some street tree situations.

CULTURE:

Transplants readily as a small or large specimen. Grows in shade, but for best autumn color plant in full sun. Very tolerant of a variety of soils, it prefers slightly acid and moist

JERRY PAVIA

conditions. Tolerant of ozone but not highly polluted areas. Leaves will develop chlorosis in high-pH soils. Relatively pest and disease free. Cutting-grown plants are preferable, as grafted plants often develop incompatibilities as they age.

VARIETIES AND RELATED SPECIES:

'October Glory' — Reaches 40 to 50 feet tall with an oval-round habit. The lustrous, dark green leaves persist long into the fall and eventually turn a brilliant orange-red. In parts of the country that nor-

mally don't have good fall color this cultivar has exhibited fine color, particularly in the South.

'Red Sunset' — Develops orange to red fall color before 'October Glory'. It is pyramidal to round in outline. Grows 45 to 50 feet tall with a spread of 35 to 40 feet and makes a great street tree. Considered by many to be the best cultivar of red maple.

HARDINESS ZONE
3 to 9

NATIVE HABITAT:
From Newfoundland to Florida west to Minnesota, Oklahoma and Texas

OUTSTANDING FEATURES:

Considered by many to be the "granddaddy" of trees for fall color, the sugar maple sets the autumn landscape ablaze with brilliant combinations of yellow, orange and red. This picturesque shade tree reaches 60 to 75 and up to 120 feet at maturity with a spread equal to two-thirds its height. In New England this tree is the source of sap for making maple syrup in late winter.

HABIT AND USE:

In its youth the habit is upright to oval becoming broadly rounded at maturity. Although somewhat intolerant of urban conditions its outstanding fall color and majestic habit make it still worth using as a street tree where road salt is not used excessively and as a specimen on larger properties. Effective as a shade tree in home landscapes, parks and campuses. The sugar maple is superior in every sense of the word to the Norway maple, *Acer platanoides.*

CULTURE:

Prefers well-drained, moderately moist and fertile soil. It is pH adaptable but will not tolerate salt, heat or compacted soils. It will grow in partial shade. The biggest problem

TIM BOLAND

with sugar maples is leaf scorch caused by drought.

VARIETIES AND RELATED SPECIES:

Subspecies *nigrum* — Has drooping leaf lobes and greater heat and drought tolerance, particularly in the Midwest.

'Green Mountain' — Heat-tolerant cultivar with dark green, leathery foliage that has good scorch resistance.

The fall color is yellow to orange to orange-red.

'Legacy' — Has a dense crown of thick, dark leaves turning to yellow-red or red in the fall. It is resistant to drought and is the superior cultivar in the South.

HARDINESS ZONE
4 to 8

NATIVE HABITAT:
Eastern Canada to Georgia, Alabama, Mississippi and Texas

Aesculus x *carnea*
RED HORSE CHESTNUT

ROBERT M. HAYS

PARENTAGE:
pavia x *hippocastanum*

OUTSTANDING FEATURES:
This deciduous tree reaches 20 to 40 feet tall with an equal spread. Spectacular in spring, when eight-inch clusters of scarlet flowers appear with the fresh new foliage. The leaves are lustrous, dark green and palmately compound (like a hand). More resistant to leaf blotch than *A. hippocastanum*, whose leaves turn a rusty brown by mid-summer.

HABIT AND USE:
Pyramidal when young, round-headed at maturity. Excellent as a flowering lawn specimen. Highly preferable to other horse chestnuts because of disease resistance.

CULTURE:
Grows in full sun to light shade, preferring moist, well drained, acid soil.

VARIETIES AND RELATED SPECIES:
'Briottii' — Deeper red-colored and larger (ten-inch) flower clusters.

HARDINESS ZONE
5 to 8

NATIVE HABITAT:
Hybrid

OUTSTANDING FEATURES:

This is truly a tree for all seasons. A harbinger of spring, it is covered with two- to three-inch white flowers in late April. The newly appearing leaves have an elegant, glistening, wooly texture. In the summer the small fruits turn black and sweet and are quickly devoured by the nearest gardener or, more likely, the nearest flock of birds. In the fall the rounded leaves turn fiery tones of yellow, gold, orange and red. Winter highlights the attractive, smooth gray bark. Named for the bloom time coinciding with the shad run in New England.

HABIT AND USE:

Because of its suckering habit, it is most effective as a

HARDINESS ZONE

3 to 7

PAUL W. MEYER

multiple-stemmed plant grown in a clump, but it can also be grown as a small, single-stemmed tree. Its ultimate height is 6 to 20 feet. Especially appropriate in a native garden, including a bog garden (its native habitat is often boggy). Great for smaller properties, patio plantings, in masses or as a foundation planting.

CULTURE:

It will perform well in many soil types, but prefers full sun to shade and well-drained, acid soil. Grows in most situations and requires very little pruning. Occasionally it suffers from rust, fire blight and powdery mildew.

VARIETIES AND RELATED SPECIES:

'Cumulus' — A distinct upright-oval habit makes this useful as a street tree or a single-trunked specimen. Fleecy white flowers. Grows 20 to 30 feet tall with half the spread. 'Robin Hill' — A possible hybrid with pale pink flowers. Grows 20 to 30 feet tall with half the spread.

NATIVE HABITAT:
Maine to Florida along the coast, west to Iowa

OUTSTANDING FEATURES:

Widely planted in southern Florida, this beautiful deciduous tree bears lavender to purple flowers that resemble small orchids in winter and early spring. Its distinctive two-lobed leaves resemble the print of an ox-hoof.

HABIT AND USE:

Growing to 20 feet tall with an umbrellalike habit, the medi-

HARDINESS ZONE

10

RUTH SOFFER

um-sized flowering tree makes an excellent street, patio, lawn or park tree, planted as a single specimen or in groups.

CULTURE:

Will thrive in full sun and ordinary soil. Minimal maintenance is required. Some pruning is needed to shape or limit the size. Fertilizing helps in poor soils.

VARIETIES AND RELATED SPECIES:

'Candida' — Pure white, orchidlike flowers.

NATIVE HABITAT:
China, India and Burma

Betula nigra
RIVER BIRCH

OUTSTANDING FEATURES:

This species has attractive, exfoliating bark that reveals inner tints of gray-brown to cinnamon. A vigorous grower, it reaches 30 to 40 feet in 20 years and ultimately 40 to 70 feet with a spread of 40 to 60 feet. The dark green leaves can turn a good yellow in the fall. The stems are an attractive reddish brown.

HABIT AND USE:

Pyramidal when young, the canopy at maturity is open and rounded. The tree thrives in hot climates, can be used in very wet situations, is the most disease resistant of the

LARRY ALBEE

birches and is good for erosion control. Effective as a single specimen, in masses, in natural areas and as a street tree. Can be used as a single- or multiple-stemmed tree.

CULTURE:

Grows in sun. An adaptable tree, it tolerates heat but

prefers moist soils with a pH of 6.5 or below. It may develop chlorosis in soils with a high pH. Resistant to the bronze birch borer which kills so many white-barked birches.

VARIETIES AND RELATED SPECIES:

'Heritage' — Selected for its outstanding bark which has white, tan, cream and peach-white tones. Beautiful every month of the year, this tree grows quickly to an effective landscape size. Best alternative to the short-lived birches. Winner of the Pennsylvania Horticultural Society Gold Medal Award.

HARDINESS ZONE
4 to 9

NATIVE HABITAT:
Massachusetts to Florida, west to Minnesota and Kansas

Callistemon citrinus
LEMON BOTTLEBRUSH

OUTSTANDING FEATURES:

This small evergreen tree grows 20 to 25 feet tall. It blooms throughout the year with two- to four-inch long spikes of red bottlebrushlike flowers at the ends of the branches. The heaviest flowering is December through March and throughout the summer. The small, narrow foliage smells of lemons when bruised.

RUTH SOFFER

HABIT AND USE:

Makes a beautiful, fine-textured, small tree when trained for a treelike habit. At the northern edge of its hardiness range, plant it in a

tub or container and protect it in winter. Can be trained as a standard.

CULTURE:

Tolerates heat, some cold and adverse soils. Grows best in full sun.

VARIETIES AND RELATED SPECIES:

'Splendens' — Brilliant carmine-red flowers are twice as large as the species.
'Red Cascade' — Abundant rosy-red flowers.

HARDINESS ZONE
9 to 10

NATIVE HABITAT:
Australia

Carpinus caroliniana
AMERICAN HORNBEAM, IRONWOOD

OUTSTANDING FEATURES:

This deciduous, native tree is grown for its smooth, tight, sinewy, slate-gray bark. A slow grower (one foot per year), it typically reaches 20 to 30 feet tall with an equal spread at maturity. The very dark green, oblong leaves turn yellow, orange and scarlet in the fall. The interesting pendulous clusters of fruit are eaten by many species of birds.

E. MEYERS

HABIT AND USE:

This highly adaptable tree is round in habit. Can be grown as a single- or multi-stemmed specimen. When grown with multiple stems it seems most fitting in a natural landscape. It can be used as a medium-sized shade tree or understory tree where a tough, long-lived plant is desired.

CULTURE:

It prefers moist, rich, slightly acid soil but will tolerate drier soils, as well as periodic flooding. Grows in sun and heavy shade. Plant a container-grown or balled-and-burlaped specimen in the spring.

HARDINESS ZONE
3 to 9

NATIVE HABITAT:
Nova Scotia to Minnesota and south to Florida and Texas

Carya ovata
SHAGBARK HICKORY

OUTSTANDING FEATURES:

A great North American native that should be more widely used in landscapes. This picturesque tree grows 60 to 80 feet, and has distinctive, attractive gray bark that flakes off in long, narrow plates. The compound, bright green summer foliage turns rich golden yellow with brown tones in fall. The fruit is edible and sweet.

PAUL W. MEYER

CULTURE:

It is adaptable to a wide range of soils but prefers well-drained, alluvial soils and full sun. Not susceptible to any major pest and disease problems, but can be difficult to transplant because of a deep tap root.

VARIETIES AND RELATED SPECIES:

Good fruiting cultivars are available.

HABIT AND USE:

This beautiful upright tree with a tall straight trunk makes an excellent specimen tree for the large landscape. Can be effective as a street planting. Good in a natural setting.

HARDINESS ZONE
4 to 8

NATIVE HABITAT:
Quebec to Minnesota, south to Georgia and Texas

Celtis occidentalis
COMMON HACKBERRY

OUTSTANDING FEATURES:

This is a good hardy tree for the plains and prairie states. It withstands adverse conditions from extreme cold to open exposed areas to wet flood plains. It grows 40 to 60 feet and up to 100 feet with an equal spread. The lustrous green leaves turn yellow in the fall. The bark is gray with wartlike chunks along the trunk. The dark purple fruits attract birds and wildlife.

HABIT AND USE:

The mature crown is broad-

HARDINESS ZONE
2 to 9

RUTH SOFFER

topped with ascending branches. Attracts a variety of wildlife. A good specimen or street tree for the harshest of conditions. Highly adaptable and good for city plantings.

CULTURE:

It prefers rich, moist soils but

tolerates dry to heavy, sandy or rocky, acid or alkaline, wet or very dry soils, urban conditions and wind. It is susceptible to witches' broom, powdery mildew and hackberry nipple gall, which may disfigure but not harm the tree.

VARIETIES AND RELATED SPECIES:

'Prairie Pride' — Uniform, compact oval crown and thick, lustrous, dark green foliage with no witches' brooms. Rapid upright growth.

NATIVE HABITAT:
From Quebec to Manitoba, south to North Carolina, Alabama, Georgia and Oklahoma

Cercidiphyllum japonicum
KATSURATREE

OUTSTANDING FEATURES:

This aristocrat is beautiful in every sense of the word. The new foliage has hints of reddish-purple and soon turns bluish green. In the fall the color is bright yellow with touches of apricot and brown. Foliage on some specimens has a distinct brown sugar odor on warm autumn days. This vigorous tree grows at least two feet per year, reaching an ultimate height of 60 to 100 feet with sometimes even greater spreads.

HARDINESS ZONE
4 to 8

PAUL W. MEYER

HABIT AND USE:

Pyramidal when young, becoming broad-spreading as it matures. It is beautiful as a multiple-stemmed tree,

as a single specimen for a large area, as a single-stemmed tree for residential properties and parks and as a street tree.

CULTURE:

Grows in sun or part shade. Prefers rich, moist, well-drained soil. The best fall color occurs in an acid soil. Pest and disease free.

VARIETIES AND RELATED SPECIES:

'Pendula' — A graceful, weeping form growing to 25 feet.

NATIVE HABITAT:
China and Japan

Cercidium floridum
PALO VERDE

OUTSTANDING FEATURES:

A small tree to 30 feet with an attractive, smooth, blue-green bark. The compound foliage is a handsome gray. Masses of striking yellow flowers are produced in four-inch long racemes April to July.

HARDINESS ZONE
9

KEN DRUSE

HABIT AND USE:

An excellent small-flowering specimen tree in arid regions.

CULTURE:

Needs heat and dryness. Best established when planted from a container.

NATIVE HABITAT:
Arizona, southern California and northwest Mexico

Cercis canadensis
REDBUD

OUTSTANDING FEATURES:

One of the most beautiful of the early spring-flowering trees. The small, one half-inch long flowers are reddish-purple in bud opening to rosy-pink with a purplish tinge, covering the naked black stems in March to April. The elegant heart-shaped leaves clothe the stems and in the fall turn a fine yellow. In six years it will grow seven to 10 feet. At maturity reaches 20 to 30 feet tall with a spread of 25 to 35 feet.

HABIT AND USE:

This small tree, single- or multi-stemmed, should have a place in every garden. It seems most fitting dotted along the edge of a native woodland, but does well in a mixed shrub border as a small understory tree. It

HARDINESS ZONE
3 to 9

PAUL W. MEYER

branches close to the ground with ascending branches in an upright arching habit. Beautiful with the native flowering dogwood.

CULTURE:

Tolerates many soil types, acid or alkaline, and full sun or light shade but prefers moist, well-drained, rich soils. Little pruning is required. Canker and verticillium wilt can make it short-lived in some areas.

VARIETIES AND RELATED SPECIES:

Var. *alba* — An elegant white-flowered form.

'Forest Pansy' — The new foliage is bright red fading to purple. An excellent foliage accent plant. Rose-pink flowers.

C. reniformis 'Oklahoma' — A wine-red flowered selection with lustrous green foliage. Native from Texas to New Mexico, this is an excellent form for southern gardens.

NATIVE HABITAT:
New Jersey to north Florida, west to Missouri and Texas and northern Mexico

Chilopsis linearis
DESERT WILLOW, FLOWERING WILLOW

OUTSTANDING FEATURES:

This 20 foot tall deciduous tree has slender, one-inch long willowlike leaves. The fragrant, bell-shaped flowers are borne in short terminal racemes throughout the summer. Each individual flower is lavender to white with two yellow stripes in the throat.

RUTH SOFFER

CULTURE:

It naturally grows in the dry parts of the Southwest. Thrives in sun. Best grown in sandy or well-drained soils. Withstands wind and tolerates drought and environmental stresses.

VARIETIES AND RELATED SPECIES:

'Burgundy' — Burgundy, trumpet-shaped flowers from spring through summer.

HABIT AND USE:

Slender upright branches form a rounded crown. A useful plant in warm and dry climates as a specimen or in group plantings. A good, tough, summer-flowering tree for arid areas.

HARDINESS ZONE

8

NATIVE HABITAT:
Texas, southern New Mexico and southern California to Mexico

Chionanthus virginicus
WHITE FRINGETREE

OUTSTANDING FEATURES:

One of the finest spring-flowering trees. In May, before the leaves emerge, the plant is covered with six- to eight-inch long, fleecy panicles of flowers that are slightly fragrant. Reaches 12 to 20 feet at maturity with an equal spread. The leaves are bold, up to eight inches long, and turn golden in the fall. In August and September the black berries are borne in abundance, attracting birds to feast.

PAUL W. MEYER

HABIT AND USE:

This broadly rounded small tree has a very open habit. Be patient: this is one of the last trees to leaf out in the spring. It can be grown as a single- or multiple-stemmed tree. It is suitable as a patio tree, in lawns, naturalized, in urban plantings or in masses.

CULTURE:

This very adaptable plant prefers deep, moist, acid, fertile soil in full sun to part shade. No pruning is required. In its native habitat it is often found along stream banks and swamps. Grows in wide pH range. Somewhat susceptible to leaf spot, canker and powdery mildew.

VARIETIES AND RELATED SPECIES:

Chionanthus retusus (Chinese fringetree) — This upright, rounded tree reaches a height of 15 to 25 feet. In May showy, fleecy white flowers cover the tree. Foliage is leathery and lustrous. Blue fruits borne August to October are very ornamental. Withstands urban conditions. Tolerant of heat. Native to China, Korea and Japan. Zone 6 to 8.

HARDINESS ZONE

4 to 9

NATIVE HABITAT:
Southern New Jersey to Florida and Texas

OUTSTANDING FEATURES:

One of the showiest flowering trees for southern California. The large tubular flowers range in color from clear pink to dark magenta, appearing from September to February followed by capsules that pop open, releasing silky floss. The bright green trunk is studded with black spines, providing year-round interest. Reaches 40 to 60 feet with an equal spread.

HABIT AND USE:

This outstanding flowering tree is too big for the small garden. It makes a fine specimen tree for the large landscape, park or campus.

CULTURE:

Thrives in full sun. Will survive below freezing in well-drained soil with reasonable fertility. Best not to plant over a sidewalk, for the fleshy flow-

ROBERT M. HAYS

ers can be rather slippery when they fall.

HARDINESS ZONE

9

VARIETIES AND RELATED SPECIES:
'Angel' — An elegant white-flowered form.

NATIVE HABITAT:
Brazil and Argentina

OUTSTANDING FEATURES:

This architectural, broadleaf evergreen reaches 40 to 60 feet with an equal spread. The new growth is bronze-red, turning to lustrous dark green. In May the greenish white, fragrant flowers are borne in two- to three-inch long panicles. Very fast growing, ultimately 50 feet with an equal spread.

RUTH SOFFER

HABIT AND USE:

In youth it is round headed, maturing to wide spreading. It is a good, dense evergreen shade tree for warm climates.

The fruits can be messy, so be sure to site this plant where that won't be a problem. Use as a specimen or street tree.

CULTURE:

Prefers acid soil, sandy or clay loam. It will tolerate dry conditions. Leaves turn yellow when exposed to wind during cold weather. Susceptible to root rot and verticillium, though neither is serious.

HARDINESS ZONE

9 to 10

NATIVE HABITAT:
Japan and China

ROBERT M. HAYS

OUTSTANDING FEATURES:

A tree for all seasons. In spring the white flowers are borne in profusion in eight- to 14-inch long, drooping, fragrant, pendulous, wisterialike panicles. The compound, bright green leaves provide a fine texture in the summer and turn golden yellow in the fall. The winter bark is a beautiful smooth gray, similar to that of the American beech.

HABIT AND USE:

Reaching 30 to 35 feet with a spread of 40 to 55 feet, this tree has a very distinct upward vase shape. It is the perfect shade tree for any size property, especially when planted near patios and terraces.

CULTURE:

Prefers well-drained, rich soils that are slightly acid. It will bleed if pruned in the spring. Sometimes develops weak crotches which in turn affect the structural durability of the tree. It has no pest and disease problems.

VARIETIES AND RELATED SPECIES:

'Rosea' — Pink flowered form.

NATIVE HABITAT:
North Carolina to Kentucky and Tennessee

HARDINESS ZONE
4 to 8

Cornus florida
FLOWERING DOGWOOD

OUTSTANDING FEATURES:

An aristocrat of small, flowering trees. At maturity reaches 30 to 40 feet with an equal spread; typically, it reaches 20 feet. In April and May the tiny green flowers are surrounded by four white bracts that make up the showy part of the flower. The fall color is excellent, varying from red to purple. The glossy red fruits may be abundant and are very attractive.

HABIT AND USE:

The branching habit is flat-topped with picturesque spreading horizontal branches. In the landscape a combination of the white and pink bracted forms makes a daz-

RUTH SOFFER

zling spring display. Is also effective in natural gardens and patios, and in winter gardens because of its branching pattern and its bark which resembles alligator skin.

CULTURE:

Prefers acid, well-drained soil with organic matter, and partial shade. Not pollution tolerant. On the East Coast lower branch dieback caused by

anthracnose is devastating garden plants and wild stands. Borer can also be a problem.

VARIETIES AND RELATED SPECIES:

'Pluribracteata' — Creamy white, double-flowered form. 'Eddy's White Wonder' — Large-flowered cross between the native East and West Coast dogwoods (*florida* x *nuttalii*). Good for the Pacific Northwest.

C. x *rutgersensis* — A new hybrid between *florida* x *kousa* that flowers midway between the two parents. Appears to be resistant to dogwood dieback.

HARDINESS ZONE
5 to 9

NATIVE HABITAT:
Massachusetts to Florida, west to Ontario, Texas and Mexico

Cornus kousa
KOUSA DOGWOOD

OUTSTANDING FEATURES:

Kousa dogwoods provide ornamental interest throughout the year. In June the stalked flowers with creamy white bracts rise above the dark green foliage, covering the branches. The flowers persist for up to six weeks and fade to an attractive light pink. The fruits, which look like oversized raspberries, are abundant in August and September. The fall foliage is a striking red, purple or scarlet. The bark is stunning year-

PAUL W. MEYER

round: a mottled pattern of grays, tans and browns. This tree will reach 20 to 30 feet at maturity with an equal spread.

HABIT AND USE:

The habit is a distinct, bold, broad vase shape with good strong horizontal lines and a stunning winter silhouette. Use as an outstanding small

specimen tree, as a patio plant, to attract birds, in a winter garden or in masses in a large landscape.

CULTURE:

Prefers a pH of 4.5 to 6.4, acid, well-drained, sandy soil rich in organic matter, and a sunny location. It is more drought tolerant than the native dogwood. Does not do well in areas with high summer heat.

VARIETIES AND RELATED SPECIES:

'Milky Way' — A very floriferous and heavily fruiting selection.
'Summer Stars' — Blooms for six weeks. Red-purple fall color.

HARDINESS ZONE
4 to 8
Does not do well in southern heat.

NATIVE HABITAT:
Japan, Korea and China

Corylus colurna
TURKISH HAZEL

OUTSTANDING FEATURES:

Makes a picturesque medium-sized, deciduous shade tree with handsome summer foliage. At maturity it will reach 40 to 50 feet tall with a spread of one third to two thirds the height. In the spring it is covered with narrow, two- to three-inch long, pendulous, golden catkins. Valued for its winter interest, the bark flakes away, revealing tan, pale brown and orange-brown bark beneath.

HABIT AND USE:

A slow-growing tree with a broadly pyramidal habit at maturity, with branches that elegantly descend to the ground. It can be grown as a single- or multi-stemmed tree. Effective as a specimen tree, patio tree, foundation planting and street tree. Very pest and disease free.

CULTURE:

Thrives in hot summers and cold winters. Tolerates adverse conditions, including dry situations, heavy soil and wind. Plant in full sun.

JUDITH D. ZUK

HARDINESS ZONE
4 to 7

NATIVE HABITAT:
Southeast Europe, west Asia

Cotinus obovatus
AMERICAN SMOKETREE

OUTSTANDING FEATURES:

In June and July masses of soft, six- to ten-inch long plumes of small, delicate green flowers are borne, creating a smokelike effect. Flowers turn a rosy color as the summer progresses. One of the best trees for fall color, the five-inch, obovate, blue-green leaves turn yellow, orange and blazing red in autumn. The plated gray bark is pleasing in winter.

JUDITH D. ZUK

HABIT AND USE:

This handsome small tree will reach 20 to 30 feet at maturity with a rounded head. Great in a native garden, it is equally at home in a city garden or a patio or as a lawn specimen.

CULTURE:

Grows in sun to part shade. Prefers well-drained, loamy, limestone soils. Tolerates wind, drought and compaction.

HARDINESS ZONE
5 to 8

NATIVE HABITAT:
Southeastern United States

Crataegus crus-galli
COCKSPUR HAWTHORN

OUTSTANDING FEATURES:

This small tree reaching 20 to 30 feet with an equal spread is appealing in every season. For seven to 10 days in May it is covered with two- to three-inch wide clusters of white flowers. In the fall the narrow, glossy, dark green leaves turn bronze-red to purple. The deep red fruits become effective in September and last into the late fall and winter.

HABIT AND USE:

This broad-rounded, low-branched tree has very archi-

tectural spreading horizontal branches. Most cockspur hawthorns develop two-inch long thorns which can cause injury, so avoid planting in highly trafficked areas. Good

as a single specimen or in mass plantings, as a screen or hedge.

CULTURE:

Grows in full sun. Adaptable to many soils, pHs and city conditions. Susceptible to fire blight, rust, scab, powdery mildew, cedar hawthorn rust and leaf blotch miner, as are most hawthorns.

VARIETIES AND RELATED SPECIES:

Var. *inermis* — A thornless variety with the same features as the species.

HARDINESS ZONE
4 to 7

NATIVE HABITAT:
Quebec to North Carolina and Kansas

Crataegus phaenopyrum
WASHINGTON HAWTHORN

OUTSTANDING FEATURES:

A plant for all seasons, this is the last hawthorn to flower. For seven to ten days in early June it is covered with two- to three-inch clusters of white flowers. In the fall the lustrous, dark green leaves turn orange to purple to scarlet. The ornamental fruits ripen to a bright, glossy red in September and October and persist all winter. At maturity the tree reaches 25 to 30 feet with an equal spread.

HABIT AND USE:

The habit is dense and rounded. Very thorny. Most effective as a single specimen or in masses, as a hedge or for screening. Provides winter interest in the garden.

CULTURE:

Adaptable to many soils, pHs and city conditions. Will tolerate windy conditions and poor soil. Susceptible to fire blight and cedar apple rust.

HARDINESS ZONE
4 to 8

NATIVE HABITAT:
Virginia to Alabama and Missouri

Crataegus viridis
GREEN HAWTHORN

OUTSTANDING FEATURES:

An outstanding small tree. In mid-May two-inch wide clusters of white flowers appear. In the fall the lustrous, dark green leaves turn to purple and scarlet. Its best attribute is its one quarter-inch fruits which ripen to an orange-red in September and persist throughout the winter. At maturity reaches 20 to 35 feet tall.

HABIT AND USE:

The habit is rounded, spreading to a vase shape. It makes a fine small specimen tree, or can be planted in masses. An excellent plant for winter interest.

CULTURE:

Best in full sun. Tolerates city conditions and a variety of soils. Less susceptible to rust than the other hawthorns.

VARIETIES AND RELATED SPECIES:

'Winter King' — Outstanding for winter color when the striking orange-red fruits are set off by the silver-gray bark which gets patches of orange-brown with age. Excellent specimen tree. Winner of the Pennsylvania Horticultural Society Gold Medal Award.

HARDINESS ZONE
4 to 7

NATIVE HABITAT:
Maryland and Virginia to Florida and west to Illinois, Iowa and Texas

---

Elaeagnus angustifolia
RUSSIAN OLIVE

OUTSTANDING FEATURES:

Valued for its narrow, silvery foliage, this small, thorny tree reaches 12 to 15 feet tall with an equal spread. A durable plant in very cold climates. The undersides of the leaves are silver, giving the entire plant a silvery cast.

HABIT AND USE:

The silver-foliaged plant makes a good accent in a white garden. It is also effective as a hedge. Salt tolerant, it can be used along highways or the seacoast. Use with discretion; can be invasive.

CULTURE:

Will tolerate any soil, seacoasts, drought and alkaline conditions. Does well in full sun with a light sandy soil. Can be kept vigorous with occasional pruning. Better in dry climates than in wet. Susceptible to verticillium and canker.

HARDINESS ZONE
2 to 7

NATIVE HABITAT:
South Europe to west and central Asia and the Himalayas

Eucalyptus ficifolia
RED-FLOWERING GUM

OUTSTANDING FEATURES:

The best of the red-flowered eucalyptus. Masses of red to pink flowers in six- to seven-inch clusters cover the tree in July and August. In California it blooms twice a year, spring and fall. Reaching 30 to 50 feet in height, this evergreen has six-inch, leathery, glossy green leaves.

RUTH SOFFER

HABIT AND USE:

The tree has a dense habit with a rounded crown. It is very effective as a street tree, windbreak or specimen, in groves or by the seashore.

CULTURE:

Withstands heat and drought although it prefers adequate water. Too much water and humidity, however, can cause physiological edema.

HARDINESS ZONE
9 to 10

NATIVE HABITAT:
West Australia

Evodia daniellii
KOREAN EVODIA, BEBE TREE

OUTSTANDING FEATURES:

A fine medium-sized, summer-flowering tree. This fast-growing tree reaches a height of 25 to 50 feet with an equal spread. The nine- to 15-inch long, compound leaves are fine textured. Small white flowers beloved by bees are borne in great profusion in four- to six-inch clusters from June to August. The ripening clusters of tiny fruit turn bright red and contrast nicely with the dark green foliage. The smooth gray bark is beechlike.

HABIT AND USE:

This broadly rounded tree grows well in the South, Midwest and East. It is very effective as a garden specimen,

ROBERT M. HAYS

shade or street tree. It is highly ornamental when few other trees are in bloom.

CULTURE:

Full sun. Prefers well-drained, moist, fertile soil. Adaptable to most soils and pHs. No serious pest and disease problems.

HARDINESS ZONE
4 to 8

NATIVE HABITAT:
Northern China and Korea

PAUL W. MEYER

OUTSTANDING FEATURES:

An aristocrat among the big specimen trees. In cultivation it reaches 50 to 70 feet, but in the wild it may reach 100 to 120 feet with an equal spread. Its picturesque leaves are dark green in summer and turn golden bronze in the fall. In the winter the massive branches and smooth, silvery trunk are exposed.

HABIT AND USE:

In the southeastern United States the American beech outperforms the European beech. The sturdy, bold trunk and densely pyramidal, spreading crown make it one of the most splendid of all specimen trees for large properties, parks and golf courses. The only drawback is that little will grow in the dense shade it casts.

CULTURE:

It prefers moist, well-drained soil with a pH of 5 to 6.5. Prefers full sun but will grow in partial shade. It will not withstand wet or compacted soils and is susceptible to leaf spots, powdery mildew, bleeding canker and beech bark disease.

HARDINESS ZONE
3 to 9

NATIVE HABITAT:
New Brunswick to Ontario, south to Florida and Texas

Fagus sylvatica
EUROPEAN BEECH

OUTSTANDING FEATURES:

Like the American beech, this elegant tree is slow growing with a very stately outline. The leaves are somewhat rounded and lustrous dark green, turning golden brown in the fall. At maturity the tree reaches 50 to 60 feet tall by 35 to 45 feet wide. The smooth gray bark has been compared to elephant hide.

HABIT AND USE:

The habit is densely pyramidal to rounded. Space is

JERRY PAVIA

needed to show this tree off properly. Use as a specimen or as a park or campus tree. Also excellent as a clipped hedge.

CULTURE:

Prefers moist, well-drained soil with a pH of 5 to 6.5. Full sun is required for best growth.

VARIETIES AND RELATED SPECIES:

'Asplenifolia' — A graceful cut-leaved form with a fern-like foliage that turns golden brown in fall.
'Atropunicea' — Striking new purple leaves in spring turn to purple-green in summer.
'Pendula' — A sculptural, weeping form.

HARDINESS ZONE
5 to 7

NATIVE HABITAT:
Europe

Franklinia alatamaha
FRANKLINIA

OUTSTANDING FEATURES:

A highly ornamental late-summer bloomer. It can reach as much as 30 feet tall, but usually is 10 to 20 feet with a spread of six to 15 feet. The bark is gray with white vertical striations. The obovate, five- to six-inch long leaves turn orange to red in the fall, and the autumn color persists quite late. In July and August the plant is covered with three-inch wide, white flowers with yellow centers, which resemble those of the

ROBERT M. HAYS

camellia, making franklinia a prized tree.

HABIT AND USE:

It is grown most effectively as a multiple-stemmed plant with an open, airy habit. Very effective in naturalized plantings, as a specimen in

small areas such as courtyards or in mixed borders.

CULTURE:

Best flowering and fall color in sun. Best planted in moist, acid, well-drained soil high in organic matter. Better in the north of its range than in the south. It will tolerate moderately alkaline soils. Susceptible to fusarium wilt.

HARDINESS ZONE
5 to 8

NATIVE HABITAT:
Once native to the Alatamaha River in Georgia, now extinct in the wild

Fraxinus americana
WHITE ASH

OUTSTANDING FEATURES:

A beautiful tree in fall when the dark green, compound leaves turn shades of yellow, purple and maroon. Reaches 50 to 80 feet with an equal spread. The growth rate is moderate at one to two feet per year.

HABIT AND USE:

This ash is vigorous and suffers from very few pest and disease problems. In youth it is oval in habit, becoming round as it gets older. It makes an excellent shade, specimen or

HARDINESS ZONE
3 to 9

street tree. Superior ornamentally to the green ash.

CULTURE:

Performs best in deep, moist, well-drained soil in full sun. It is pH adaptable. May be susceptible to leaf rusts, leaf spots, cankers, ash borer, fall webworm and scale, but vig-

orously growing trees perform well.

VARIETIES AND RELATED SPECIES:

'Autumn Purple' — Pyramidal rounded outline. Reddish-purple fall color lasts for two to four weeks. Reaches 45 feet with a spread of 60 feet at maturity. 'Autumn Applause' — A densely branched oval form with reliable maroon fall color. Forty feet tall by 25 feet wide. 'Greenspire' — Narrow upright habit, with dark orange autumn leaf color.

NATIVE HABITAT:
From Nova Scotia to Minnesota, south to Florida and Texas

Fraxinus pennsylvanica
GREEN ASH

OUTSTANDING FEATURES:

This deciduous shade tree reaches 50 to 80 feet tall with a spread of 25 to 40 feet. The compound leaves turn a lovely yellow in the fall. It tolerates adverse conditions better than the white ash.

HABIT AND USE:

At maturity the habit is upright and spreading. Grows a vigorous two to three feet per year. It makes a very good street tree or

HARDINESS ZONE
3 to 9

shade tree. A good choice for the plains states. Best to grow seedless varieties.

CULTURE:

It will grow almost anywhere and tolerates high pH, salt, drought and poor soil. Does best in full sun.

Susceptible to the same problems as white ash.

VARIETIES AND RELATED SPECIES:

'Marshall's Seedless' — Glossy, dark green foliage turning yellow in the fall. Forty feet tall and seedless. More vigorous and less insect prone than the species. 'Dakota Centennial' — An extremely hardy, globe-shaped, seedless selection.

NATIVE HABITAT:
Nova Scotia to Manitoba, south to northern Florida and Texas

Ginkgo biloba
GINKGO, MAIDENHAIR TREE

PAUL W. MEYER

OUTSTANDING FEATURES:

This grand tree reaches 80 feet tall with a variable spread from 30 to 80 feet. The distinctive bright green, fan-shaped leaves turn a rich golden yellow in the fall.

HABIT AND USE:

The habit is pyramidal when young, becoming spreading and picturesque as the tree matures. An excellent city tree, it makes a great specimen tree, street tree and espalier. Be sure to get a male selection; the female fruits are messy and malodorous.

CULTURE:

Grows in almost any situation, tolerating air pollution, a wide pH range and salt. Quite heat tolerant, it performs well in the South. Grows best in sandy, deep, moderately moist soil in full sun. It is pest and disease free.

VARIETIES AND RELATED SPECIES:

'Autumn Gold' — Broad conical male form, 50 feet tall and 30 feet wide, with beautiful golden fall color.

'Princeton Sentry' — A good upright male form, tapering to a narrow pyramid.

HARDINESS ZONE
4 to 9

NATIVE HABITAT:
Eastern China

Gleditsia triacanthos var. *inermis*
HONEYLOCUST

PAUL W. MEYER

OUTSTANDING FEATURES:

This fine-textured tree produces very light shade. The bright green, compound leaves are six to eight inches long with very tiny leaflets that turn yellow in fall. Grows 30 to 70 feet with an equal spread.

HABIT AND USE:

The spreading crown makes a lovely silhouette. The growth rate is two feet per year. Bordering on overused, but it does make a good street tree or lawn tree because its light shade allows grass to grow all the way up to the trunk.

CULTURE:

Withstands a wide range of conditions but prefers rich, moist soils and full sun. A good urban tree as it tolerates drought, high pH and salt. Susceptible to cankers, witches' brooms and webworm. Does not perform well in the South.

VARIETIES AND RELATED SPECIES:

'Continental' — A seedless selection with dark blue-green leaflets, a narrow crown and stout branches. Sixty to 70 feet tall.

'Imperial' — Thirty to 35 feet selection with spreading branches and rounded habit.

'Skyline' — Forty-five feet by 35 feet wide with strong growing, ascending branches. More upright than most.

HARDINESS ZONE
4 to 9

NATIVE HABITAT:
From Pennsylvania to Nebraska and south to Texas and Mississippi

ROBERT M. HAYS

OUTSTANDING FEATURES:

Its elegant summer foliage and statuesque habit make the Kentucky coffeetree a grand tree. The compound leaves are 36 inches long and 24 inches wide with handsome bluish green leaflets and yellow fall color. A slow-growing tree, it will reach up to 90 feet tall with a spread of 40 to 50 feet. The nearly black trunks of male trees have an architectural outline that seems to have been made for the front of a haunted house.

HABIT AND USE:

Vertically ascending branches form an oval crown. An excellent tough tree for big lawns, city parks, campuses and golf courses. It makes a good specimen tree with summer texture and winter interest. Cleaning up the pods from the female trees can be a nuisance.

CULTURE:

Prefers deep, rich, moist soils but adapts to a wide range of soils, drought and city conditions. Is not susceptible to any pest and disease problems. An undemanding, beautiful tree.

NATIVE HABITAT:
From New York to Pennsylvania to Minnesota, Nebraska, Oklahoma and Tennessee

HARDINESS ZONE
4 to 8

Halesia tetraptera (H. carolina)
CAROLINA SILVERBELL

OUTSTANDING FEATURES:

This elegant tree is grown for its profusion of flowers in late April and early May. The white, bell-shaped flowers are one half- to three quarter-inch long, in clusters of two to five. The tree will ultimately reach 30 to 80 feet by 20 to 25 feet. The bark is gray with white striations.

HABIT AND USE:

Can vary from a narrow head to a broad, rounded crown.

HARDINESS ZONE
5 to 8

RUTH SOFFER

Tolerant of city conditions, it can be used as a specimen, patio or shade tree. Also excellent in the shrub and woodland border as a single- or multi-stemmed tree. Beau-

tiful when white flowers are set off by an evergreen background.

CULTURE:

Grows best in rich, well-drained, moist soil high in organic matter with a pH of 5 to 6; becomes chlorotic in soils with a high pH. Very pest and disease resistant. Prefers full sun or semi-shade.

NATIVE HABITAT:
From West Virginia to Florida to east Oklahoma

Hovenia dulcis
JAPANESE RAISINTREE

OUTSTANDING FEATURES:

The attractive, heart-shaped leaves of this deciduous tree are four to six inches long and glossy. The bark exfoliates in thin, narrow strips, revealing a rusty underside. In June and July the tree is covered with two- to three-inch wide clusters of white, sweetly fragrant flowers. At maturity this tree reaches 40 to 50 feet with two thirds the spread.

HABIT AND USE:

Makes a beautiful upright tree with a rounded crown at maturity. A perfect patio or small lawn tree that deserves wider use. As they mature in

HARDINESS ZONE
5 to 8

ROBERT M. HAYS

the fall, the fleshy branches of the inflorescences become sweet like raisins and are valued by Oriental peoples.

CULTURE:

Very adaptable to a variety

of soil conditions, sun or shade and a wide pH range and tolerates wind.

NATIVE HABITAT:
China

Ilex x attenuata
HYBRID HOLLY

PARENTAGE:

cassine x *opaca*

OUTSTANDING FEATURES:

This handsome group of hybrid hollies has dark green, narrow, evergreen leaves with slightly spiny margins. The abundant, deep red berries last throughout the winter. Grows 20 to 25 feet tall.

HABIT AND USE:

Valued for its fine texture and slender pyramidal habit, it is excellent as a specimen or for massing, hedging or screen-

RUTH SOFFER

ing. Responds well to pruning. Choose a female clone for ornamental fruits. Not as reliably hardy in the north as the native American holly.

CULTURE:

Grows best in moist, loose, acid, well-drained soil in full sun or partial shade.

VARIETIES AND RELATED SPECIES:

'Foster #2' — The best of the Foster hybrids. Twenty to 25 feet tall with a narrow habit, dark green foliage and bright red fruits.

'East Palatka' — Bright red, one quarter-inch wide fruits in abundance. Looser habit than 'Foster #2', and less hardy for northern gardens.

HARDINESS ZONE
7 to 9

NATIVE HABITAT:
Hybrid

Ilex opaca
AMERICAN HOLLY

OUTSTANDING FEATURES:

This native evergreen holly has spiny, dark green, three-inch long leaves. The small red fruits ripen in September and last throughout the winter. On older specimens the bark is smooth and gray. At maturity will reach 40 to 50 feet tall with a spread of 18 to 40 feet.

HABIT AND USE:

The habit is densely pyramidal, becoming irregular and picturesque at maturity. Can be used for screening, massing, foundation plantings, hedges and cutting for holiday wreaths. A male plant is

PAUL W. MEYER

needed nearby for fruit production on the female plant.

CULTURE:

In Illinois the American holly has withstood temperatures of -20 to -25 degrees F. For best growth plant in moist, loose, acid, well-drained soil in part shade to full sun. Avoid dry winds and soils with a high pH. Susceptible to holly leaf miner, holly berry midge and scale.

VARIETIES AND RELATED SPECIES:

The cultivars of American holly are almost limitless. A few good ones are:
'Boyce Thompson Xanthocarpa' — A heavy-fruiting, yellow-berried selection.
'Jersey Knight' — A male form with dark green leaves and a handsome habit. Good pollinator.
'Jersey Princess' — Female, with lustrous, dark green leaves, a handsome form and abundant red fruits.
'Old Heavy Berry' — Large, dark green leaves and heavy crops of dark red fruits.

HARDINESS ZONE
5 to 9

NATIVE HABITAT:
From Massachusetts to Florida, west to Missouri and Texas

Ilex vomitoria
YAUPON

OUTSTANDING FEATURES:

A very adaptable native evergreen for southern gardens. The one to two inch leaves of the Yaupon are small, lustrous and dark green. A fast grower, it reaches an ultimate height of 15 to 20 feet. The small scarlet fruits are borne in great quantities and last into the spring. Older trees can be limbed up to expose the white to grayish bark.

HABIT AND USE:

A fine-textured small tree. The mature habit is upright, irregularly branched and very picturesque. Very effective in the winter garden, as a screen or hedge, in masses or as a topiary. It responds well to pruning.

CULTURE:

Very adaptable, it will withstand quite dry to extremely wet conditions and salt spray. Suffers from no pest and disease problems.

VARIETIES AND RELATED SPECIES:

'Shadows Female' — Dark green, with almost round leaves and bright red fruits. Excellent as a topiary.

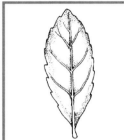

HARDINESS ZONE
7 to 10

NATIVE HABITAT:
From Long Island, New York, to central Florida and west Texas

---

Jacaranda mimosifolia
JACARANDA

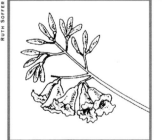

OUTSTANDING FEATURES:

A good tree for southern California and Florida. Prized for its funnel-shaped, lavender-blue flowers borne in profusion in eight inch clusters from April to June. The doubly compound leaves are made up of many tiny leaflets, giving it a ferny texture. Grows to 50 feet tall.

HARDINESS ZONE
10

HABIT AND USE:

This broadly rounded, spreading, medium-sized tree makes an excellent street, lawn and park tree in the warm tropics. Briefly deciduous, it is a good choice where winter sun and summer shade is desired.

CULTURE:

Thrives in any well-drained soil in sun. Not salt tolerant. Responds well to pruning.

NATIVE HABITAT:
Brazil and northwest Argentina

Koelreuteria bipinnata
CHINESE FLAME TREE

OUTSTANDING FEATURES:

This fast-growing tree reaches 30 to 40 feet at maturity. The large compound leaves are dark green and have good overall texture. Blooming later than most trees, it produces large showy panicles of fragrant yellow flowers from August to September, followed by papery capsules that turn rose-pink. These color-

ful, very ornamental fruits last for three to five weeks.

HABIT AND USE:

One of the few yellow-flowered trees, it has an open, spreading crown. A great, late-flowering small tree. Particularly useful for small gardens and patios.

CULTURE:

Grows best in full sun or filtered shade. It will withstand wind, drought, heat and air pollution and adapts to a wide range of soil conditions. No pest or disease problems.

HARDINESS ZONE
6 to 9

NATIVE HABITAT:
China

Koelreuteria paniculata
GOLDENRAIN TREE

OUTSTANDING FEATURES:

A fast-growing, summer-flowering tree reaching 30 to 40 feet with an equal spread. In July the very showy, 12- to 15-inch long, upright sprays of yellow flowers bloom, followed by attractive papery-brown seed capsules. The flowers make a bold contrast with the dark green, compound foliage which turns yellow, gold and orange in fall.

HABIT AND USE:

At maturity the habit is round to spreading. It could have some applications as a small street tree, but is best as a lawn or patio tree or specimen tree in a small gar-

den. Valued for its summer flowers and handsome foliage.

CULTURE:

Highly adaptable and useful in cities. Tolerates a wide range of soils. Withstands drought, heat, wind, alkaline soils and air pollution and has no serious pest and disease problems.

VARIETIES AND RELATED SPECIES:

'Fastigiata' — A strongly upright tree, reaching 25 feet with a six foot spread. Useful where a narrow flowering tree is desired.

HARDINESS ZONE
5 to 9
(perhaps 4)

NATIVE HABITAT:
China, Japan, Korea

ROBERT M. HAYS

OUTSTANDING FEATURES:

The summer-flowering crape myrtles are outstanding from July to September when the flowers are borne in six- to eight-inch long panicles of white, pink, purple and deep red. The smooth gray bark exfoliates into striking mosaic patterns of gray, brown and cream. A small tree, it can reach 15 to 25 feet in height.

HABIT AND USE:

The crape myrtles are most attractive as multi-stemmed trees used as patio or specimen trees, or in the back of a border. They take well to heavy pruning and can be made into a hedge. The exquisite bark makes them suitable for the winter garden. They thrive in the South, performing well in more northern areas. Because they flower on new growth, they can be used as shrubs in colder areas where stems die back but the roots are hardy.

CULTURE:

Prefer well-drained soil and full sun. May be susceptible to powdery mildew, black spot, aphids, Florida wax scale.

HARDINESS ZONE
7 to 9

VARIETIES AND RELATED SPECIES:
L. fauriei — Exceptional rusty brown bark. Twenty- to 25-foot tall, multi-stemmed tree with white flowers. Fast growing. Zone 6.

The U.S. National Arboretum has introduced many mildew-resistant hybrids between *indica* x *fauriei* of varying heights and colors. Some good ones include:
'Muskogee' — Twenty-one feet tall by 15 feet wide with glossy green foliage that turns red in the fall. Profuse lavender to pink flowers in four- to ten-inch long panicles from July through September. Mildew resistant. Shiny light gray to tan bark.
'Natchez' — Twenty-one feet tall by 21 feet wide. Dark cinnamon, sinuous, mottled, exfoliating bark. Dark green foliage turns orange to red in the fall. The pure white flowers are borne in six- to twelve-inch long panicles from June to September. Resistant to aphids.

NATIVE HABITAT:
China and Korea

Liquidambar styraciflua
AMERICAN SWEETGUM

OUTSTANDING FEATURES:

This handsome street tree is best noted for its star-shaped, four- to seven-inch wide, lustrous dark green leaves that turn brilliant shades of yellow, purple and red in the fall. It can grow 60 to 120 feet tall with two-thirds the spread. The corky bark is picturesque in the winter.

HABIT AND USE:

The tree is densely pyramidal when young and rounded when mature. The growth rate is moderate. The dry, spiny, round fruits can be messy

RUTH SOFFER

when they fall from December to April. Excellent as a lawn, park or street tree in a suburban setting where the fruits won't be a problem. Needs room for root development. One of the best trees for fall color in southern California.

CULTURE:

Tolerant of a wide range of conditions, it performs best in deep, moist, slightly acid soils in full sun. Does not do well in the city where the roots are constricted. Relatively pest free but may be susceptible to bleeding necrosis, sweetgum webworm, scale and chlorosis in high-pH soils.

VARIETIES AND RELATED SPECIES:

'Rotundiloba' — A fruitless cultivar with rounded, not pointed, dark green leaves that turn rich reddish purple to yellow in fall.

HARDINESS ZONE
6 to 9

NATIVE HABITAT:
From New York, Ohio, Indiana, Illinois and Missouri south to Florida, Texas and Mexico

---

Liriodendron tulipifera
TULIP TREE

OUTSTANDING FEATURES:

A pyramidal tree when young, this aristocrat is one of the tallest of all shade trees, up to 150 feet at maturity. The bark is a beautiful smooth gray with striations. The three to four inch, yellow-orange, tulip-shaped flowers appear after the distinctive bright green leaves unfold. Fall color is buttery yellow.

HARDINESS ZONE
4 to 9
(withstood -25 degrees Fahrenheit in Minnesota)

JOANNE PAVIA

HABIT AND USE:

Makes an excellent fast-growing, large shade, lawn, park or campus tree. It can also be used as an overstory tree in a natural woodland. Not for the small garden.

CULTURE:

Prefers deep, moist, well-drained loam in full sun but is not fussy about pH. Do not plant as a street tree or near a driveway as aphids on leaves secrete a sticky "honeydew" which falls on cars.

NATIVE HABITAT:
Massachusetts to Wisconsin, south to Florida and Mississippi

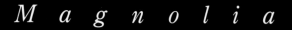

M a g n o l i a

T he magnolias include some of the most magnificent of flowering trees. Their conspicuous, sweetly scented flowers are among the showiest in temperate areas. Many cultivars and hybrids are now available to gardeners, ranging from the ten- to 15-foot tall Little Girl Hybrids 'Ann', 'Betty', 'Jane', 'Judy', 'Pinkie', 'Randy', 'Ricki' and 'Susan' with late, pink to purple flowers to the glamorous 'Galaxy', a 20 to 30 foot, pyramidal tree with deep reddish purple flowers late in April.

Most magnolias have thick, fleshy root systems and are best transplanted in early spring. The following are some of the best ornamental species and hybrids.

Magnolia denudata
YULAN MAGNOLIA

OUTSTANDING FEATURES:

One of the most beautiful species, this tree is covered with fragrant, five- to six-inch wide, ivory, saucer-shaped blooms in early April, followed by five-inch long leathery leaves. The pewter-gray bark is handsome in winter.

HABIT AND USE:

Irregularly rounded in habit, it reaches 30 to 40 feet, with an equal spread. Easily grown as a single-stemmed plant.

HARDINESS ZONE
5 to 8

PAUL W. METER

Effective specimen, shade or lawn tree in the small garden.

CULTURE:

Prefers sun or some shade and rich moist soil. Does not tolerate extreme moisture or drought and hot, dry, windy areas.

VARIETIES AND RELATED SPECIES:

x 'Elizabeth' — A striking

yellow-flowered hybrid of *acuminata* x *denudata* developed by the Brooklyn Botanic Garden. The fragrant, creamy flowers, which appear in late April to May, withstand the late-spring cold. Fast growing, it flowers at a young age and grows rapidly to a rounded, 30 foot tree. Winner of the Pennsylvania Horticultural Society Gold Medal Award.

NATIVE HABITAT:
Central China

Magnolia grandiflora
SOUTHERN MAGNOLIA

OUTSTANDING FEATURES:

This aristocratic broad-leaved evergreen is justly famous worldwide for its beautiful leaves and flowers. The lustrous, leathery, five- to ten-inch leaves are dark green above and reddish brown and pubescent below. The large, creamy white, fragrant flowers occur heavily in June and sporadically through the summer. The decorative fruits make good additions to Christmas wreaths.

HABIT AND USE:

This densely pyramidal magnolia reaches 60 to 80 feet at maturity with a spread of 30 to 50 feet. In the South it is an unequaled specimen tree. More

HARDINESS ZONE
7 to 9

TIM BOLAND

northern gardeners should consider one of the hardy cultivars. Useful as a specimen, shade tree or a street tree (in warm climates), or for screening or espaliering (on a north or west wall in northern climates).

CULTURE:

Prefers rich, porous, acid, well-drained soil. In the North (Zone 7) choose a spot protected from winter wind and sun. Pest and disease free.

VARIETIES AND RELATED SPECIES:

'Edith Bogue' — The most

cold hardy of the cultivars (hardy in Montclair, New Jersey). Thirty feet tall by 15 feet wide, with a pyramidal habit.
'Hasse' — Noted for its dense, upright habit and lustrous, dark green leaves. Smaller than the species. Good for screening. Promising for Zone 6.
'Little Gem' — A small, 20-foot tall plant with smaller dark green leaves with rusty brown undersides. A heavy bloomer throughout the summer. Very compact. Not reliable in Zone 7.
'Samuel Sommer' — Rapidly growing 30 to 40 foot tree with large (ten to 14 inch) flowers. Best in Zones 8 and 9.

NATIVE HABITAT:
North Carolina to Florida and Texas

JOANNE PAVIA

PARENTAGE:

denudata x *liliiflora*

OUTSTANDING FEATURES:

A popular magnolia, this beautiful flowering tree reaches 20 to 30 feet tall at maturity with an equal spread. The spectacular white or pink to rose-purple flowers cover the tree in early- to mid-April before the leaves appear. The bark is a handsome smooth gray. Fuzzy buds and architectural habit add winter interest.

HABIT AND USE:

The broad-rounded tree is best grown as a multi-stemmed plant where the low branches can spread. Plant in masses or as a single specimen.

CULTURE:

This fleshy-rooted tree prefers rich, porous, acid, well-drained soil in full sun. It is mostly pest and disease free. Sapsucker holes may disfigure bark but are not harmful to the tree. Flowers may be susceptible to late-spring frosts.

VARIETIES AND RELATED SPECIES:

'Alexandrina' — A free-flowering late variety with deep rose-pink flowers flushed white inside.

'Brozzonii' — An elegant, late, white-flowered cultivar.

'Lennei' — One of the latest and largest-flowered forms. Goblet-shaped rose-magenta blossoms in late April.

HARDINESS ZONE
5 to 9

NATIVE HABITAT:
Hybrid

Magnolia tomentosa (M. stellata)
STAR MAGNOLIA

PAUL W. MEYER

OUTSTANDING FEATURES:

The earliest magnolia to flower, this delicate small tree is covered with many-petalled, starry white flowers in early April before the four-inch leaves appear. At maturity it reaches 15 to 20 feet with an equal spread.

HABIT AND USE:

A useful early-flowering, densely rounded, multi-stemmed, large shrub or small tree. Effective in borders, foundation plantings, near a patio, as a lawn specimen or in groupings. Beautiful underplanted with crocus or squills.

CULTURE:

Prefers sun to light shade with a rich, well-drained, acid soil. Will tolerate some wind and drought. Suffers from no pest and disease problems.

VARIETIES AND RELATED SPECIES:

'Rosea' — The pale pink-flowered form of this lovely small tree.

'Royal Star' — Has fragrant white flowers that open later than the species. A handsome rounded plant.

M. x *loebneri* — A hybrid between *tomentosa* and *kobus*. Excellent small to medium tree. 'Merrill' is a beautiful fast-growing, 25 foot, broadly pyramidal cultivar with showy fragrant white flowers in early April. 'Leonard Messel' is covered with small blush-pink flowers in mid-April.

HARDINESS ZONE
5 to 6

NATIVE HABITAT:
Japan

Magnolia virginiana
SWEET BAY MAGNOLIA

ROBERT M. HAYS

OUTSTANDING FEATURES:

One blossom of this native tree fills the air with its perfume. The two to three inch, lemon-scented flowers appear in May to June and sporadically through the summer. In the North this tree is deciduous and reaches 15 to 25 feet tall with a spread of ten to 15 feet. In the South it is nearly evergreen and reaches 60 feet tall. The handsome five-inch long, oblong leaves are lustrous dark green above. When the wind blows the silvery white undersides flicker in the light.

HABIT AND USE:

This open upright tree can be grown as a single- or multi-stemmed tree. Excellent as a patio tree where the extremely fragrant blossoms can be appreciated. Useful for wet sites and for small- to medium-sized gardens.

CULTURE:

Prefers sun to part shade and acid, loamy soils. Does well in wet, almost swampy conditions. It does not like dry situations and will become chlorotic in high-pH soils.

VARIETIES AND RELATED SPECIES:

The variety *australis* and the cultivar 'Henry Hicks' are both evergreen to Zone 6.

HARDINESS ZONE
5 to 9

NATIVE HABITAT:
Massachusetts to Florida and Texas

LARRY ALBEE

Technically, crabapples are apple trees with fruits less than two inches in diameter. They are valued for their great range of ornamental flowers, fruits and habits. All the crabs are deciduous and reach 15 to 25 feet tall. Their habits vary from low-mounding to upright or vase-shaped. Flowering occurs from April to early June, in colors ranging from white, pink and rose to carmine and red. Fruits are very ornamental and vary in color from deep red to golden yellow. Crabapples will thrive in a variety of soil conditions but prefer well-drained, moist, acid soil with a pH of 5 to 6.5 and full sun. Generally, they require little pruning, and all pruning should be done by early June before flower buds are set for the next year. The crabs are susceptible to a wide variety of pest and disease problems, including fire blight, cedar apple rust, apple scab, canker, scale, borers and aphids. Be sure to choose pest-resistant selections.

Malus floribunda
JAPANESE FLOWERING CRABAPPLE

OUTSTANDING FEATURES:

A picturesque, fragrant, flowering tree. The buds of this crab are deep pink to red, opening to one and one half-inch white flowers in May. The three quarter-inch yellow and red fruits are attractive to birds. Grows to 15 to 25 feet with an equal spread.

HABIT AND USE:

The broad-rounded, densely branched tree is beautiful planted in masses, as a lawn specimen or as a patio tree. The small, white-flowered crabapple with showy fruits attracts wildlife.

CULTURE:

Slightly susceptible to scab and powdery mildew and moderately susceptible to fire blight.

HARDINESS ZONE
5 to 8

NATIVE HABITAT:
Japan

Malus hybrids:

'CALLAWAY' — One of the best disease-resistant, white-flowered crabs for southern gardens. Buds are pink and open white, followed by persistent, large maroon fruits. Reaches 15 to 25 feet tall with a picturesque rounded head. Slightly susceptible to mildew and fire blight.

'CENTURION' — Highly disease-resistant, pink-flowered crab. Red buds open rose-red, followed by glossy red fruits. The 25 foot tree with upright branching and a 15 to 20 foot spread is useful in small gardens and as a street tree.

'DONALD WYMAN' — One of the best fruiting crabs for winter interest. The

Malus hupehensis
TEA CRABAPPLE

OUTSTANDING FEATURES:

One of the most beautiful crabs. In May the picturesque armlike branches are covered with fragrant flowers. The deep pink buds open to white. The fruits begin yellow and turn red. They persist into late winter, providing food for flocks of cedar waxwings, robins and other birds. The

RUTH SOFFER

fall foliage color is yellow to copper. Grows to 24 feet with an equal spread.

HABIT AND USE:

The vase-shaped habit is very architectural, with long branches reaching up and out from the trunk. Attractive year-round, it is an excellent specimen tree for the small or large garden.

CULTURE:

Tolerates wind and drought. Slightly susceptible to fire blight.

HARDINESS ZONE

4 to 8

NATIVE HABITAT:

China

Malus sargentii
SARGENT CRABAPPLE

OUTSTANDING FEATURES:

One of the smallest crabapples. The buds are red and open to one-inch wide, white, fragrant flowers in May. The fruit is bright red and attractive to birds. Grows to ten feet tall with a ten to 15 feet spread.

PAUL W. MEYER

and wide-spreading. Effective in masses or singly in a shrub border or as a specimen where a small, shrubby tree is desired.

CULTURE:

Slightly susceptible to scab, fire blight and leaf spot.

HARDINESS ZONE

4 to 8

HABIT AND USE:

The habit is dense-mounding

NATIVE HABITAT:

Japan

---

glossy, bright red fruits persist long into the winter. Pink buds open to single white flowers. A large spreading tree reaching 20 feet tall and 25 feet wide at maturity, it is resistant to scab, cedar apple rust and fire blight and slightly susceptible to powdery mildew.

'RED JADE' — A graceful weeping variety introduced by BBG. Deep pink buds open to one and one half-inch white flowers along the pendulous branches of this 15 foot tree. The attractive glossy red fruits are enjoyed by birds. Ideal for the small garden as an accent plant. Moderately susceptible to scab and powdery mildew.

Nyssa sylvatica
TUPELO, BLACK GUM, SOUR GUM

JOANNE PAVIA

OUTSTANDING FEATURES:

One of the most picturesque of all the shade trees, this disease-resistant native is noted for its brilliant autumn color. The three- to six-inch long, lustrous leaves turn yellow to orange to brilliant scarlet early in the fall. Dark blue fruits are quickly eaten by birds. The handsome bark looks like alligator hide.

HABIT AND USE:

The habit is pyramidal when young and spreading with an irregular, flat-topped crown when mature. Thirty to 50 feet tall with a 30 foot spread. Excellent tree for naturalizing, or as a shade or specimen tree. Acceptable as a street tree in residential but not heavily polluted areas.

CULTURE:

Prefers moist, well-drained, deep, acidic soil. Tolerant of almost swampy conditions but not high pH. Will grow in full sun or shade.

HARDINESS ZONE
3 to 9

NATIVE HABITAT:
From Maine to Ontario and Michigan to Florida and Texas

O x y d e n d r u m   a r b o r e u m
SOURWOOD, SORREL TREE

OUTSTANDING FEATURES:

One of the most striking small trees for fall color. In cultivation it usually reaches 25 to 30 feet tall with a spread of 20 feet. The elliptic, lustrous, dark green leaves turn brilliant scarlet to purple in the fall. Also valued for its white, urn-shaped, fragrant flowers borne in June to July in ten-inch, drooping panicles in great profusion. The cream-colored persistent fruit capsules make a dazzling contrast with the vivid fall foliage.

HARDINESS ZONE
4 to 9

JERRY PAVIA

HABIT AND USE:

An upright tree growing 25 to 30 feet with a 20 foot spread. This small tree can't be beat for its outstanding blooms and fall color. Plant in a small garden, as a specimen tree or in a native garden.

CULTURE:

Prefers acid, moist, well-drained soil in full sun or partial shade. Best fall color occurs in full sun with a pH of 5.5 to 6.5.

NATIVE HABITAT:
From Pennsylvania and Ohio south to Florida, Mississippi, and Louisiana.

P i s t a c i a   c h i n e n s i s
CHINESE PISTACHIO

OUTSTANDING FEATURES:

A tough, drought-resistant tree with good fall color for southern and desert gardens. At maturity this medium-sized tree reaches 35 feet tall with an equal spread. The compound ten-inch long, lustrous, dark green leaves turn a brilliant orange-red in fall. In the South this is the closest any tree gets to the fall color of sugar maples. The bark has touches of orange and salmon.

HARDINESS ZONE
6 to 9

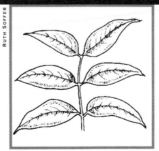
RUTH SOFFER

HABIT AND USE:

The growth rate is moderately fast. The mature habit is oval to rounded. This fine-textured tree makes a good small shade, patio, lawn,

foundation or specimen tree. Its tolerance of poor, droughty soils makes it a good candidate for urban situations.

CULTURE:

A very adaptable tree, tolerating a wide range of conditions. Thrives in moist, well-drained soils in full sun but tolerates drought. No pest or disease problems.

NATIVE HABITAT:
Central and western China

PARENTAGE:

orientalis x *occidentalis*

OUTSTANDING FEATURES:

A tough shade tree with considerable winter interest. This large tree reaches 75 to 100 feet with an equal spread. Beautiful exfoliating bark reveals a mosaic of whites, tans, forest greens and grays. Foliage resembles large matte-green maple leaves.

HABIT AND USE:

Pyramidal when young, developing to a large, open, wide-spreading tree. Best used in open areas in parks and large landscapes where it can fully develop. Responds well to pruning. Highly tolerant of urban conditions, making it a popular street tree.

CULTURE:

Does best in full sun or light shade in deep, rich, moist, well-drained soils. Adaptable, tolerating high-pH soils, pollutants and very moist to dry city conditions. Anthracnose can cause defoliation; canker-stain can be serious.

VARIETIES AND RELATED SPECIES:

'Bloodgood' — An improved selection showing good resistance to anthracnose and tolerance of compaction, heat and drought. Fast growing, with dark green summer foliage. *P. occidentalis* — This native is lovely growing along woodland edges and streamsides where its outstanding winter beauty can be appreciated. Its massive trunk has beautiful exfoliating bark revealing a ghostly mosaic of whites, tans and grays.

HARDINESS ZONE
5 to 9

NATIVE HABITAT:
Hybrid

Populus deltoides
EASTERN COTTONWOOD

OUTSTANDING FEATURES:

This extremely fast-growing tree (up to four to five feet per year) reaches a height of 75 feet with a 50 foot spread. Very winter hardy and recommended for the plains states. The lustrous green leaves can show good yellow fall color in some areas. The tufted seeds have a cottony appearance.

HABIT AND USE:

Pyramidal in youth, spreading to vase-shaped at maturity. A weak-wooded, sometimes messy tree, this species is best suited for colder climates in the United States or for naturalizing along streams and river bottoms.

CULTURE:

Prefers moist soil but toler-

HARDINESS ZONE
2 to 9

RUTH SOFFER

ates dry soils with a wide pH range. The cottonwood is short-lived, rarely ever reaching 70 years old.

VARIETIES AND RELATED SPECIES:

'Noreaster' (*deltoides* x *nigra*) — A cottonless male that

grows four feet per year. Canker resistant.

NATIVE HABITAT:
From Quebec to North Dakota and south to Texas and Florida

Prosopis glandulosa
HONEY MESQUITE

OUTSTANDING FEATURES:

A drought-resistant native tree for southwestern gardens. The foliage is bright green and feathery. In November the honey mesquite is covered with yellow-orange flowers that are attractive to bees.

HARDINESS ZONE
8

KEN DRUSE

HABIT AND USE:

A medium-sized tree, to 50 feet, with upright branches forming a symmetrical crown.

Makes a good specimen or patio tree for desert and semi-desert regions. Best to choose a thornless selection.

CULTURE:

Drought resistant. Will not survive temperatures below 0 degrees Fahrenheit.

NATIVE HABITAT:
Texas, southeast Arizona, southern California and northern Mexico

The flowering cherries are most beautiful in early spring when they produce their delicate single to double, pure white to deep rose flowers. There is a cherry for every garden situation, from the shrubby 'Hally Jolivette' to the narrow, upright 'Amanogawa' to the large, weeping *Prunus subhirtella*. The small fruits are inconspicuous, appearing after the leaves and quickly eaten by birds.

Cherries prefer full sun. They are susceptible to borers, scale and a variety of other insects and diseases, and are relatively short-lived. But those 50 or so years are filled with unequalled spring beauty.

P r u n u s x 'O k a m e'
OKAME CHERRY

WALTER HOLT

PARENTAGE:

incisa x *campanulata*

OUTSTANDING FEATURES:

A first-class small flowering tree, this upright cherry reaches a mature height of 25 feet with a 15 foot spread. The dark red buds open to clear pink flowers, often at the end of March. After the petals drop the deep red calyx gives a rosy glow. The two-inch

leaves turn yellow to orange to red in the fall. This fast-growing tree flowers at an early age. A Pennsylvania Horticultural Society Gold Medal winner.

HABIT AND USE:

Upright and oval at maturity, the 'Okame' cherry makes a splendid small specimen, patio, foundation or street tree. One of the best and earliest flowering trees.

CULTURE:

Prefers well-drained, slightly acidic soil in full sun.

HARDINESS ZONE
5 to 8

NATIVE HABITAT:
Hybrid

P r u n u s   s e r r u l a t a
JAPANESE FLOWERING CHERRIES

CHRISTINE M. DOUGLAS

PARENTAGE:

The important cultivars are hybrids of unknown parentage.

OUTSTANDING FEATURES:

The last cherries to flower, these trees are covered with single to double blossoms from mid-April to early May. The five-inch, elliptic, dark green leaves turn bronze, yellow and red in fall. These trees reach 20 to 35 feet with an equal spread.

HABIT AND USE:

The mature habit is vase-shaped to rounded and spreading. These are ideal candidates for the small garden, patio and lawn as well as

street plantings. A memorable sight in spring.

CULTURE:

Prefers full sun to light shade and well-drained soil with adequate moisture. Susceptible to canker, borer, scale, tent caterpillar and ice storm damage.

VARIETIES AND RELATED SPECIES:

'Amanogawa' — A curious, narrow, 20-foot tall variety with a five-foot spread. Pale pink flowers in late April.

'Sekiyama' ('Kwanzan') — The most popular and probably the hardiest of the double-flowering types. Bronze fall color. Rounded vase-shape at maturity. Deep pink blossoms in late April.

'Shirotae' — A beautiful white-flowered cherry with fragrant, semi-double blossoms in mid-April. A 20 to 25 foot tree.

'Shogetsu' — A small, rounded, 18 foot tree with blush-pink flowers in mid- to late-April.

HARDINESS ZONE
5 to 8
(depending on the cultivar)

NATIVE HABITAT:
Japan

CHRITINE M. DOUGLAS

OUTSTANDING FEATURES:

This species has produced many worthy cultivars with pink to white flowers in early- to mid-April. The ultimate height is 20 to 40 feet with a spread of 15 to 30 feet. Does well in the East, Midwest and South.

HABIT AND USE:

Wide-spreading and rounded to pendulous, depending on the cultivar. Best as a specimen, patio or small street tree, particularly where it can be admired from a distance.

CULTURE:

This cherry prefers sun and good soil with adequate moisture and a pH of 5 to 7. May be susceptible to canker, borer, scale, virus and tent caterpillar.

VARIETIES AND RELATED SPECIES:

'Autumnalis' — Valued for its fall flowering, it produces pale pink to white flowers heavily in early April and again in the fall. A 20 to 30 foot, rounded tree.

'Hally Jolivette' — A small, 15 foot, rounded tree with double white flowers in mid-April. Ideal flowering tree for small spaces. Hybrid *subhirtella* x *yedoensis*.

'Pendula' — Weeping Higan Cherry — This graceful weeping tree blooms in early April with one half-inch wide, single, pale pink flowers. At maturity reaches 20 to 40 feet tall with a spread of 14 to 30 feet.

'Yae-shidare-higan' — A graceful weeping form with double, dark pink, abundant flowers in early April that last longer and are deeper in color than those of 'Pendula'.

HARDINESS ZONE
4 to 8

NATIVE HABITAT:
Japan

Prunus x yedoensis
YOSHINO CHERRY

PARENTAGE:

serrulata x *subhirtella*

OUTSTANDING FEATURES:

The Yoshino is the aristocrat of the cherries, a big white cloud in the spring landscape. The mildly fragrant flowers are pink in bud and open pure white in late March or early April. At maturity it reaches 40 to 50 feet tall with an equal spread. This is the famous cherry that lines the Tidal Basin in Washington, D.C.

HARDINESS ZONE
5 to 8

ROBERT M. HAYS

HABIT AND USE:

Bold and broadly spreading, developing into a picturesque crown. An excellent lawn, park and specimen tree. Old street tree plantings survive in suburbs of Washington, D.C.

CULTURE:

Prefers sun or light shade, and clay or loam soil with adequate moisture and a pH of 5 to 7. May be susceptible to canker, borer, scale, virus and tent caterpillar.

VARIETIES AND RELATED SPECIES:

'Afterglow' — A handsome pink-flowered form with yellow fall color. Upright and spreading to 25 feet tall by 25 feet wide.

NATIVE HABITAT:
Hybrid

Pyrus calleryana 'Bradford'
BRADFORD CALLERY PEAR

OUTSTANDING FEATURES:

The Bradford pear has become one of the most popular, bordering on overplanted, small flowering trees. This fast-growing tree has a mature height of 30 to 50 feet with a spread of 20 to 35 feet. In late April to May it is covered with three inch clusters of white flowers. The leaves are dark, glossy green turning scarlet to purple in the fall. In the South fall color peaks in mid to late November.

HABIT AND USE:

Pyramidal in youth, becoming

HARDINESS ZONE
5 to 8

ROBERT M. HAYS

rounded with time. A good tree for streets, lawns and foundations. Do not choose this tree for areas where it is already overused and more diversity is needed. The Bradford pear has tight branch crotches which split in older trees; other cultivars may prove sturdier over time.

CULTURE:

Prefers full sun. Adaptable to a variety of soils, dryness, pollution. Relatively pest and disease free. Some tip dieback occurs in the South from fire blight.

VARIETIES AND RELATED SPECIES:

'Aristocrat' — Better branching angles than 'Bradford'. Yellow to red fall color. Heat and cold tolerant, but susceptible to fire blight.
'Red Spire' — Stiffly pyramidal with yellow fall color. Slower growing than 'Bradford'. Susceptible to fire blight.

NATIVE HABITAT:
The species is native to Korea and China

Quercus agrifolia
COAST LIVE OAK

OUTSTANDING FEATURES:

An excellent native evergreen tree for California gardens. Dark, glossy, hollylike foliage is handsome all year long. Well adapted to wet winters and dry summers. Fifty feet tall with an equal spread.

HARDINESS ZONE

9

ALLEN HOWARD

HABIT AND USE:

A round-headed, medium- sized tree. Valuable as a shade tree in gardens, parks and commercial landscapes.

CULTURE:

An adaptable tree, best planted in full sun. Ideal for gardens in the hills and valleys of coastal California.

NATIVE HABITAT:
Coastal California

Quercus alba
WHITE OAK

OUTSTANDING FEATURES:

The native white oak is a noble specimen throughout the year, with a particularly memorable winter silhouette. The lobed, four to eight inch leaves turn orange, red, violet or purple in the fall. As it matures, the bark breaks off, creating handsome patterns of gray. The acorns are eaten by various mammals. Slow growing to 50 feet with an 80 foot spread. At maturity it can be massive: The 400-year-old Wye Oak in Maryland is 95 feet tall with a 165 foot spread.

HABIT AND USE:

Very stately. When young the white oak is pyramidal, becoming broadly rounded with wide-spreading branches. Makes a magnificent specimen or shade tree.

HARDINESS ZONE

3 to 9

TIM BOLAND

CULTURE:

Grows in many types of soil. Does best in full sun in deep, moist, well-drained soil with a pH of 5.5 to 6.5. Usually durable, long-lived and pest and disease free.

VARIETIES AND RELATED SPECIES:

Q. bicolor — The swamp white oak grows to 50 to 60 feet with an equal spread.

Broad to rounded crown. Grows naturally in low-lying swampy areas. Yellow to red-purple fall color. Native habitat ranges from Quebec to Georgia, west to Michigan and Arkansas. Good for naturalizing or as a shade tree.

NATIVE HABITAT:
Maine to Florida, west to Minnesota and Texas

Quercus imbricaria
SHINGLE OAK

JOANNE PAVIA

OUTSTANDING FEATURES:

An elegant, shiny-leaved oak. The six inch, oblong leaves are a lustrous, dark green, turning yellow to russet in the fall. At maturity the height is 50 to 60 feet with an equal spread. It is a very good oak for calcareous soils in the Midwest.

HABIT AND USE:

In youth the shingle oak is pyramidal, becoming upright and oval and finally broad-rounded in old age. It can be used as a shade, lawn, golf course, park and street tree. Can be pruned as a hedge or screen. Useful as a wind-break, as the leaves persist into the winter.

CULTURE:

Prefers moist, rich, deep, well-drained, acid soil and full sun. Tolerant of dry calcareous soils and city conditions.

HARDINESS ZONE
5 to 8

NATIVE HABITAT:
From Pennsylvania to Georgia, west to Nebraska and Arkansas

Quercus macrocarpa
BUR OAK

PAUL W. MEYER

OUTSTANDING FEATURES:

The bur oak, like the white oak, is picturesque. It is most handsome standing alone, particularly against the winter sky. The fall color is yellow to brown and not as brilliant as the white oak. The bur oak reaches 70 to 100 feet with an equal spread at maturity.

HABIT AND USE:

A very impressive large specimen tree. The crown rises from a stout straight trunk and is broad and open at maturity. Use as a single specimen to provide a large shade canopy. White tail deer, wood duck, turkey and squirrel all eat the acorns.

CULTURE:

Needs full sun. Difficult to transplant but adapts to a wide range of soils, from sandy plains to moist alluvial bottoms. Favors limestone soils; does well in dry, clay soils. The most tolerant of city conditions of all the oaks. No major pest and disease problems.

HARDINESS ZONE
3 to 8

NATIVE HABITAT:
From Nova Scotia to Pennsylvania and west to Manitoba and Texas

PAUL W. MEYER

OUTSTANDING FEATURES:

A beautiful fine-textured oak. The narrow, five inch, willow-shaped, bright green leaves turn yellow to rusty brown in the fall. In cultivation this tree will reach 40 to 60 feet tall with a spread of 30 to 40 feet.

HARDINESS ZONE
6 to 9

Considered one of the best oaks for texture and form and ease of culture.

HABIT AND USE:

Pyramidal in youth, becoming oval in maturity. Perfect shade tree for streets, lawns and parks. Because the leaves are small, relatively little raking is required in the fall.

CULTURE:

Transplants more readily than other oaks. Prefers moist, well-drained soil but will tolerate a variety of conditions. Pest and disease free.

NATIVE HABITAT:
New York to Florida and west to Missouri and Texas

Quercus rubra
RED OAK

OUTSTANDING FEATURES:

One of the best oaks for most parts of the United States. Grows a rapid two feet per year and ultimately reaches 60 to 75 feet with a spread of up to 100 feet. The dark green leaves turn red to bright red in the fall, exhibiting better fall color than the overplanted pin oak.

HABIT AND USE:

In youth the red oak is rounded, becoming broadly rounded at maturity. It is a great shade tree for lawns, streets, parks, campuses and golf courses and for naturalized plantings.

CULTURE:

Transplants readily. Does best in well-drained, acid, sandy loam in full sun. Will develop chlorosis in high-pH soils. Relatively pest and disease free.

HARDINESS ZONE
4 to 8

NATIVE HABITAT:
Nova Scotia to Pennsylvania, west to Minnesota and Iowa

Quercus shumardii
SHUMARD OAK

OUTSTANDING FEATURES:

A handsome tree that tolerates tough conditions. The six inch, lustrous, deeply lobed green leaves turn bright red in the fall. The shumard oak is very drought resistant, making it a good choice for specimen tree plantings in Oklahoma and Texas. At maturity, reaches 40 to 60 feet with an equal spread. Performs better than the pin oak because it tolerates alkaline, clay soils.

HABIT AND USE:

Pyramidal in youth, becoming rounded and spreading at maturity. A good shade tree for street, city, park and lawn.

CULTURE:

Best in sun. Extremely stress tolerant, growing in acid to alkaline, clay or sandy soils in wet and dry conditions. Some problems with oak wilt, but otherwise pest and disease free.

HARDINESS ZONE
5 to 8

NATIVE HABITAT:
Kansas to south Michigan to North Carolina, Florida and Texas

Quercus virginiana
LIVE OAK

OUTSTANDING FEATURES:

A magnificent shade tree for southern gardens. This ever-green oak has fine-textured, three-inch long, lustrous, dark green leaves. The broad-spreading tree has massive horizontal arching branches that are often covered with Spanish moss. Grows 40 to 80 feet tall with a 60 to 100 foot spread.

HABIT AND USE:

Makes a splendid shade tree for large properties, campuses and parks. The acorns are eaten by quail, turkey, squirrel and deer.

CULTURE:

Grows in any type of soil. Useful as a street tree as it tolerates compacted soil and salt spray. Root rot can be a problem in coastal areas.

HARDINESS ZONE
8 to 10

NATIVE HABITAT:
Virginia to
Florida,
west to Mexico

Salix babylonica
BABYLON WEEPING WILLOW

OUTSTANDING FEATURES:

The leaves of the Babylon weeping willow are very narrow, giving this tree an extremely delicate texture. This, in addition to its weeping habit, make the tree a fine architectural specimen in the landscape. At maturity it reaches 30 to 40 feet tall with an equal spread.

HABIT AND USE:

This willow has a short trunk with graceful weeping branches that sweep to the ground. Best used in very moist areas near rivers or ponds, not in areas where water is in short supply. The fast-growing

JERRY PAVIA

species is not hardy in New England.

CULTURE:

Thrives in moist soils and is pH adaptable. Susceptible to twig blight, canker, powdery mildew and several insects.

Also susceptible to ice and wind damage. A greedy water user, this tree should not be used in low-rainfall areas.

HARDINESS ZONE
6 to 8

NATIVE HABITAT:
China

Sassafras alhidum
SASSAFRAS

OUTSTANDING FEATURES:

A handsome native tree with bright green three-lobed, mitten-shaped leaves that turn fantastic shades of yellow, orange, scarlet and purple in the fall. The stems are an attractive bright green in autumn. At maturity the sassafras can reach 30 to 40 feet tall with a spread of 25 to 40 feet.

HABIT AND USE:

Pyramidal and irregular in

TIM BOLAND

youth, becoming flat-topped and oblong at maturity. Grows stoloniferously, therefore expansive colonies can form. Great for native plant-

ings, stabilizing soils and small gardens.

CULTURE:

Grows in full sun to part shade. Prefers moist, loamy, acid, well-drained soil. May develop chlorosis in high-pH soils. No pest or disease problems. Remove suckers if a single trunk is desired.

HARDINESS ZONE
4 to 9

NATIVE HABITAT:
From Maine to Ontario
and Michigan,
south to Florida and Texas

Sophora japonica
JAPANESE PAGODATREE, SCHOLAR TREE

OUTSTANDING FEATURES:

One of the best summer-flowering trees. The creamy white flowers are borne in 12-inch long terminal clusters from July through August. They are followed by showy, bright green pods. At maturity this tree is 50 to 75 feet tall with an equal spread. The compound foliage gives it an overall fine texture.

HABIT AND USE:

The habit is broad and round-headed and spreading at

PAUL W. MEYER

maturity. Tolerates city conditions and poor soil, making it suitable for the suburban landscape or for use as a street tree.

CULTURE:

Grows in sun to part shade in average soils. Tolerates heat and drought, and pollution. Prune in fall.

VARIETIES AND RELATED SPECIES:

'Princeton Upright'— A compact, upright form growing to 40 to 50 feet. Good where spread must be limited. 'Regent' — Selected for its fast growth rate, oval crown and glossy, deep green leaves. Flowers early, at six to eight years.

HARDINESS ZONE
5 to 8

NATIVE HABITAT:
China and Korea

Sophora secundiflora
TEXAS MOUNTAIN LAUREL, MESCAL BEAN

OUTSTANDING FEATURES:

An excellent native flowering tree for southwest gardens. This evergreen has thick, lustrous, dark shiny green compound leaves. The very fragrant violet-blue flowers are borne in wisterialike clusters in March to April. In cultivation this tree reaches 15 to 25 feet tall. The fruit is a bright red pod that matures in September.

HABIT AND USE:

A small, upright, dense tree attractive for street plantings or in the small garden as a specimen or espaliered.

ROBERT M. HAYS

CULTURE:

Prefers sun to moderate shade and alkaline soils with good drainage. Tolerates drought and air pollution but not soil compaction. No pest or disease problems.

HARDINESS ZONE
8 to 10

NATIVE HABITAT:
Texas, New Mexico and Mexico

PAUL W. MEYER

RTUH SOFFER

PAUL W. MEYER

OUTSTANDING FEATURES:

A tree with year-round interest. In May the plant is covered with white, flat-topped flower clusters. In September its showy berries turn from pinkish red and orange to scarlet and persist until the lustrous, dark green, oval leaves turn a warm orange to red. On mature trees the ultimate height is 40 to 50 feet tall with a spread of 20 to 30 feet. The smooth beechlike bark is attractive in winter.

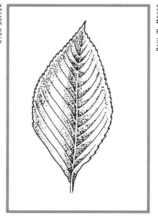

HABIT AND USE:

Pyramidal when young and oval at maturity. A handsome small specimen tree with showy flowers and impressive autumn color.

CULTURE:

Grows best in sun in well-drained soil. Tolerates a wide pH range, wind and wet conditions but not air pollution. Least susceptible of the mountain ashes to borer.

HARDINESS ZONE
4 to 7
Grows well in Minnesota

NATIVE HABITAT:
Central China, Korea and Japan

Sorbus aucuparia
EUROPEAN MOUNTAIN ASH

OUTSTANDING FEATURES:

A handsome small tree with compound, dark green leaves that turn shades of yellow, red and purple in the fall. In May three to five inch, flat-topped clusters of white flowers are borne, followed by showy orange-red fruits in the fall. Because European mountain ash is susceptible to a host of diseases in warm areas, it should be grown only in northern climates. At maturity this tree reaches 20 to 40 feet tall.

HARDINESS ZONE
3 to 6

JOANNE PAVIA

HABIT AND USE:

The upright oval tree can be an excellent fruiting, flowering and fall-color tree for northern areas. Good with an evergreen background to set off the fruit and fall foliage.

CULTURE:

Prefers well-drained loam. Does not do well in polluted areas. Susceptible to canker, borer, fire blight, rust, scab and aphids. Short-lived in areas with warm summers.

VARIETIES AND RELATED SPECIES:

'Apricot Queen' — Apricot-colored fruit.
'Cardinal Royal' — Vigorous grower with brilliant red fruits.
'Xanthocarpa' — Yellow fruits.

NATIVE HABITAT:
Europe, west Asia and Siberia

Stewartia pseudocamellia
JAPANESE STEWARTIA

OUTSTANDING FEATURES:

A summer-flowering tree with unbeatable winter interest. The bark is smooth, sinuous and exfoliating, leaving mottled patches of rust, cream, greens, gray, brown and terra cotta. At maturity the tree reaches 20 to 40 feet. In July the two and one half-inch, camellialike flowers occur over a two week period. The elliptic leaves turn wine-red to purple in the fall.

HABIT AND USE:

Pyramidal to oval at maturity.

HARDINESS ZONE
6 to 7

LARRY ALBEE

For the small garden there is no better choice. Makes a great patio or small specimen tree for any landscape.

CULTURE:

Grows in sun to part shade. Prefers moist, acid soil with a pH of 4.6 to 6.5. Does not tolerate environmental stresses. No major pest or disease problems.

VARIETIES AND RELATED SPECIES:

S. pseudocamellia var. koreana — More open, with larger flowers than the species. Bright yellow to orange-red fall color. A Pennsylvania Horticultural Society Gold Medal Plant.

NATIVE HABITAT:
Japan

PAUL W. MEYER

OUTSTANDING FEATURES:

This elegant small flowering tree produces pendulous, mildly fragrant white flowers in May to June. The oval, tapering, rich green leaves turn yellow in the fall. Grows 20 to 30 feet with an equal spread.

HABIT AND USE:

This graceful, low-branched, rounded small tree makes a fine patio, foundation and small specimen tree. Plant where you can look up into the canopy when in flower.

PAUL W. MEYER

CULTURE:

Grows in sun and part shade in zones 7 and 8. Thrives in loamy, light, well-drained soil high in organic matter with a pH of 5 to 7.

VARIETIES AND RELATED SPECIES:

'Pink Chimes' — Upright habit, with pink flowers. 'Pendula' — A graceful weeping form.

HARDINESS ZONE
5 to 8

NATIVE HABITAT:
China and Japan

PAUL W. MEYER

OUTSTANDING FEATURES:

Flowering before *Styrax japonicus*, the fragrant snowbell has fragrant white flowers borne in long, drooping clusters in May to June. The handsome habit and smooth gray bark are good for winter effect. At maturity this tree reaches 20 to 30 feet.

HABIT AND USE:

The broad spreading tree with dense ascending branches should be planted close to pathways or entrances to the home where the fragrant flowers can be enjoyed. A beautiful specimen tree.

PAUL W. MEYER

PAUL W. MEYER

CULTURE:

Does best in full sun to light shade, in acid, well-drained, moist, rich soil. No pest or disease problems.

HARDINESS ZONE
5 to 8

NATIVE HABITAT:
Japan

Syringa reticulata
JAPANESE TREE LILAC

ROBERT M. HAYS

OUTSTANDING FEATURES:

A small tree valued for its summer flowers, this lilac blooms later than most and is not as susceptible to disease. The flowers are borne in 12-inch long creamy white panicles in May in the South, June in New England and July in the Midwest. Attractive shiny, cherrylike bark adds winter interest. At maturity this lilac reaches 30 feet with a spread of 15 to 29 feet.

HABIT AND USE:

The erect rounded plant is best as a specimen or small street tree. Also effective in masses.

CULTURE:

Will tolerate drought but thrives in sun, slightly acid, well-drained soil. Susceptible to scale and borer. Prefers cool summers.

VARIETIES AND RELATED SPECIES:

'Ivory Silk' — Flowers at a young age. A compact, dense, heavy-flowering plant.
'Summer Snow' — Creamy white, very profuse flowers.

HARDINESS ZONE
4 to 7

NATIVE HABITAT:
Japan

Tabebuia chrysotricha
GOLDEN TRUMPET TREE

JERRY PAVIA

OUTSTANDING FEATURES:

This deciduous, sometimes evergreen tree grows four to five feet per year and reaches 30 to 50 feet tall. The dazzling bright yellow, trumpet-shaped flowers are borne in clusters in late March through April. The fruit is a long brown bean that persists in winter.

HABIT AND USE:

The open spreading tree is spectacular in flower during late winter to early spring. Excellent as a specimen tree for gardens and a street tree in zone 10.

CULTURE:

Thrives in rich loam and sun. Tolerates light or heavy soils and drought.

VARIETIES AND RELATED SPECIES:

Tabebuia impetiginosa 'Pink Cloud' — Brilliant deep pink flowers in late winter to early spring.

HARDINESS ZONE
9

NATIVE HABITAT:
Brazil, south Florida, Colombia and Mexico

Tilia cordata
LITTLELEAF LINDEN

OUTSTANDING FEATURES:

This vigorous shade tree has a good shape. Its distinctive heart-shaped foliage is dark green turning yellow in the fall. Inconspicuous flowers perfume the air in late June.

HARDINESS ZONE
3 to 7

HABIT AND USE:

The habit is pyramidal to oval at maturity. An outstanding street or shade tree for lawns, planters, parks and malls. It can also be trimmed as a hedge. Grows as far north as Manitoba, Canada.

CULTURE:

Prefers full sun and well-drained fertile soils. A tough city tree

that is pH adaptable and pollution tolerant. Aphids and Japanese beetles can be a problem.

VARIETIES AND RELATED SPECIES:

'Greenspire' — Maintains a single leader with strong branching. Does well under difficult conditions. Dark green foliage.

NATIVE HABITAT:
Europe

Tilia x euchlora
CRIMEAN LINDEN

PARENTAGE:

cordata x *dasystyla*

OUTSTANDING FEATURES:

This graceful hybrid is less stiff in habit than the littleleaf linden. The lustrous, dark green leaves turn yellow-green in fall. At maturity it reaches 40 to 60 feet tall with one half the spread.

HARDINESS ZONE
3 to 7

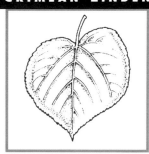

HABIT AND USE:

The lower branches skirt the ground, giving this tree a very graceful habit. Like littleleaf linden, it is excellent

for street, park, lawn and specimen plantings.

CULTURE:

Grow in full sun. Tolerant of hot, dry conditions and pollution.

VARIETIES AND RELATED SPECIES:

'Redmond' — A very hardy popular selection in the Midwest. Densely pyramidal, growing to 50 feet.

NATIVE HABITAT:
Hybrid

PAUL W. MEYER

OUTSTANDING FEATURES:

A beautiful specimen tree that reaches 50 to 70 feet with two thirds the spread at maturity. The leaves are dark green above and silver below, giving the tree a shimmering appearance when the wind blows. The fall color is a good yellow. The yellow-white flowers are inconspicuous but highly fragrant in early summer.

HABIT AND USE:

Pyramidal to oval at maturity. A very good shade tree in home gardens, parks, golf courses and commercial landscapes.

CULTURE:

Grows in sun in average soil. Tolerates wind, salt and air pollution. Somewhat susceptible to aphids, but shunned by Japanese beetles.

VARIETIES AND RELATED SPECIES:

Tilia petiolaris — Closely allied species with graceful pendulous branches that sweep the ground. An outstanding large specimen tree.

NATIVE HABITAT:
Southeast Europe and west Asia

HARDINESS ZONE
4 to 7

Ulmus crassifolia
CEDAR ELM

OUTSTANDING FEATURES:

An excellent native elm for arid conditions, this tree grows to 50 to 70 feet tall with a spread of 40 to 60 feet. The small leaves exhibit some fall color.

RUTH SOFFER

CULTURE:

Plant in sun. Will withstand drought and heavy, infertile soil. Can be susceptible to Dutch elm disease and elm leaf beetles.

HABIT AND USE:

A fine-textured tree. Used as a street and shade tree in the Southwest.

HARDINESS ZONE
7 to 9

NATIVE HABITAT:
Mississippi to Arkansas and Texas

Ulmus parvifolia
LACEBARK ELM

OUTSTANDING FEATURES:

A highly adaptable ornamental tree. The small, lustrous, dark green leaves turn yellow to reddish in fall. At maturity this elm reaches 40 to 70 feet tall with a spread of 40 feet. The growth rate is moderate to fast. The winter bark is a stunning mottled gray, brown, cream and orange.

HABIT AND USE:

This strong-wooded elm is round headed at maturity. Use in a winter garden, on a patio, in urban areas or as a street tree. It is often called the Chinese elm, however the true Chinese elm is the inferior *Ulmus pumila*.

ROBERT M. HAYS

CULTURE:

Grows in sun and shade. Adaptable to extreme soil and pH and tolerant of pollution and soil compaction. Resistant to Dutch elm disease and elm leaf and Japanese beetle.

VARIETIES AND RELATED SPECIES:

'Emerald Vase' — A large (70 feet) tree with upright spreading branches resembling the American elm.

HARDINESS ZONE
5 to 9

NATIVE HABITAT:
North and central China, Korea and Japan

ROBERT M. HAYS

OUTSTANDING FEATURES:

A handsome, graceful, vigorous shade tree. At maturity the Japanese zelkova reaches 50 to 80 feet with an equal spread. The smooth gray bark becomes mottled with creams, grays and oranges. Fall color ranges from yellow to orange, brown, red and red-purple.

HABIT AND USE:

This broadly vase-shaped plant has been used as a substitute for the disease-wracked American elm. Excellent in urban situations as a street tree, it also makes a nice specimen and shade tree.

CULTURE:

Thrives in sun in deep, moist soils but tolerates a range of pHs, pollution, wind, drought and soil compaction. Resistant to Dutch elm disease.

VARIETIES AND RELATED SPECIES:

'Green Vase' — Vase-shaped, upright arching branches. More graceful than 'Village Green'.
'Village Green' — Rapid growth, superior fall color and cold hardiness.

NATIVE HABITAT:
Japan

HARDINESS ZONE
5 to 8

RECOMMENDED *Trees* BY REGION

Lack of space prevents us from running an exhaustive list of recommended trees by region. The following is a list of ten choice trees for nine major regions of the country.

NORTHEAST

Nyssa sylvatica

Cladrastis lutea

Acer griseum Paperbark maple	*Nyssa sylvatica* Black tupelo
Betula nigra River birch	*Quercus rubra* Red oak
Cladrastis kentukea (C. lutea) Yellowwood	*Sorbus alnifolia* Korean mountain ash
Cotinus obovatus American smoketree	*Stewartia pseudocamellia* Japanese stewartia
Koelreuteria paniculata Goldenrain tree	*Syringa reticulata* Japanese tree lilac

M I D - A T L A N T I C

Acer palmatum	*Magnolia* x *soulangiana*
Japanese maple	Saucer magnolia
Betula nigra	*Malus hupehensis*
River birch	Tea crabapple
Cornus florida	*Prunus* x *yedoensis*
Flowering dogwood	Yoshino cherry
Corylus colurna	*Quercus phellos*
Turkish hazel	Willow oak
Crataegus viridis 'Winter King'	*Sophora japonica*
Green hawthorn	Japanese pagodatree

C r a t a e g u s   v i r i d i s

M a g n o l i a x *s o u l a n g i a n a*

S O U T H E A S T

Acer rubrum	*Pistacia chinensis*
Red maple	Chinese pistachio
Betula nigra	*Quercus phellos*
River birch	Willow oak
Koelreuteria bipinnata	*Quercus virginiana*
Goldenrain tree	Live oak
Magnolia grandiflora	*Ulmus parviflora*
Southern magnolia	Chinese elm
Malus 'Callaway'	*Zelkova serrata*
Flowering crabapple	Japanese zelkova

M a g n o l i a   g r a n d i f l o r a

Q u e r c u s   v i r g i n i a n a

MIDWEST

Betula nigra

Syringa reticulata

ROBERT M. HAYS

BOB HYLAND

Acer rubrum Red maple	*Malus* 'Donald Wyman' Flowering crabapple
Acer saccharum Sugar maple	*Quercus macrocarpa* Bur oak
Betula nigra River birch	*Quercus rubra* Red oak
Carpinus caroliniana American hornbeam	*Syringa reticulata* Japanese tree lilac
Fraxinus pennsylvanica Green ash	*Tilia cordata* Littleleaf linden

CENTRAL PLAINS

Cercis canadensis

Ginkgo biloba

BOB HYLAND

TIM BOLAND

Acer rubrum Red maple	*Populus deltoides* Eastern cottonwood
Celtis occidentalis Common hackberry	*Quercus rubra* Red oak
Cercis canadensis Redbud	*Sophora japonica* Japanese pagodatree
Ginkgo biloba Maidenhair tree	*Syringa reticulata* Japanese tree lilac
Gymnocladus dioicus Kentucky coffeetree	*Tilia* x *euchlora* Crimean linden

ROCKY MOUNTAINS

Acer ginnala	*Koelreuteria paniculata*
Amur maple	Goldenrain tree
Celtis occidentalis	*Populus deltoides*
Common hackberry	Eastern cottonwood
Crataegus viridis 'Winter King'	*Quercus macrocarpa*
Green hawthorn	Bur oak
Elaeagnus angustifolia	*Quercus rubra*
Russian olive	Red oak
Gleditsia triacanthos var. *inermis*	*Tilia cordata*
Honeylocust	Littleleaf linden

JERRY PAVIA

Elaeagnus angustifolia

TIM BOLAND

Koelreuteria paniculata

DESERT SOUTHWEST & TEXAS

Cercidium floridum	*Quercus virginiana*
Palo verde	Live oak
Cercis reniformis	*Prosopis glandulosa*
Redbud	Honey mesquite
Chilopsis linearis	*Sophora secundiflora*
Desert willow	Mescal bean
Pistacia chinensis	*Ulmus crassifolia*
Chinese pistachio	Cedar elm
Quercus shumardii	*Ulmus parviflora*
Shumard oak	Chinese elm

BOB HYLAND

Cercis canadensis

PAUL W. MEYER

Ulmus parviflora

Acacia baileyana

Chionanthus retusus

Acacia baileyana
Cootamundra wattle

Koelreuteria bipinnata
Goldenrain tree

Aesculus x *carnea*
Red horse chestnut

Magnolia grandiflora
Southern magnolia

Chionanthus retusus
White fringetree

Malus floribunda
Japanese flowering crabapple

Eucalyptus ficifolia
Red-flowering gum

Pistacia chinensis
Chinese pistachio

Ginkgo biloba
Maidenhair tree

Quercus agrifolia
Coast live oak

Chorisia speciosa

Cinnamonum camphora

Acacia baileyana
Cootamundra wattle

Jacaranda mimosifolia
Jacaranda

Callistemon citrinus
Lemon bottlebrush

Liquidambar styraciflua
American sweetgum

Chorisia speciosa
Floss-silk tree

Magnolia grandiflora
Southern magnolia

Cinnamomum camphora
Camphor tree

Quercus agrifolia
Coast live oak

Eucalyptus ficifolia
Red-flowering gum

Tabebuia chrysotricha
Golden trumpet tree

HARDINESS ZONE

Map

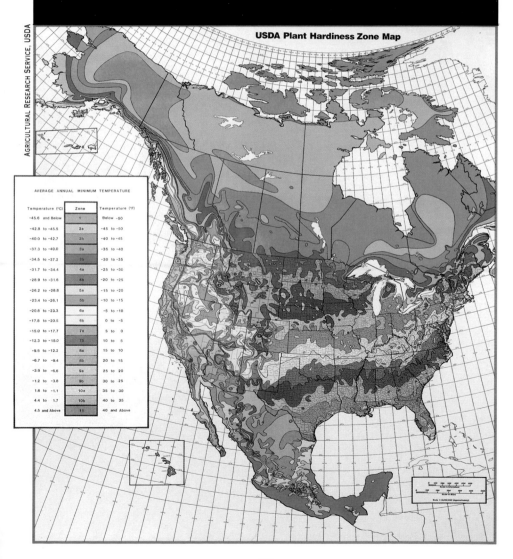

USDA Plant Hardiness Zone Map

AVERAGE ANNUAL MINIMUM TEMPERATURE

Temperature (°C)	Zone	Temperature (°F)
-45.6 and Below	1	Below -50
-42.8 to -45.5	2a	-45 to -50
-40.0 to -42.7	2b	-40 to -45
-37.3 to -40.0	3a	-35 to -40
-34.5 to -37.2	3b	-30 to -35
-31.7 to -34.4	4a	-25 to -30
-28.9 to -31.6	4b	-20 to -25
-26.2 to -28.8	5a	-15 to -20
-23.4 to -26.1	5b	-10 to -15
-20.6 to -23.3	6a	-5 to -10
-17.8 to -20.5	6b	0 to -5
-15.0 to -17.7	7a	5 to 0
-12.3 to -15.0	7b	10 to 5
-9.5 to -12.2	8a	15 to 10
-6.7 to -9.4	8b	20 to 15
-3.9 to -6.6	9a	25 to 20
-1.2 to -3.8	9b	30 to 25
1.6 to -1.1	10a	35 to 30
4.4 to 1.7	10b	40 to 35
4.5 and Above	11	40 and Above